IMMIGRATION
Is South Africa facing economic genocide?

IMMIGRATION
Is South Africa facing economic genocide?

FANA PETSOANE

This book is published by
© 2020 Fana Petsoane

ISBN 978-1-990-98013-8

FOREWORD

This short book was inspired by recent squabbles between immigrants and locals in South Africa. Hostilities could have been avoided had the state enforced existing sovereign laws to manage immigration without fear or favour. After months of raising the same issues with the Presidency, Chapter 9 institutions and a Portfolio Committee in parliament without a response, the book had to be written!

South Africa has one of the most reliable official statistical agencies in the continent that has produced many reports which are seemingly just ignored by political leaders. The current migration crisis in this country is a symptom of that ongoing negligence by senior state leaders. The constant scuffles for limited South African resources derail the intended unity of Africans due to state mismanagement of South Africa's sovereignty. The book is also intended to stimulate debate on immigration challenges in South Africa. The discussion is based on a review of local and international legislation, official statistical reports as well as official statements by local and international government leaders. A wide spectrum of journal articles and books have also been reviewed. All official legislation is quoted in italics in the text.

I am grateful to individuals who assisted editorially and otherwise in ensuring the book is published.

ACCRONYMS

ANA	-	African News Agency
AU	-	African Union
B-BBEE	-	Broad-Based Black Economic Empowerment
DEL	-	Department of Employment and Labour
DHA	-	Department of Home Affairs
DTIC	-	Department of Trade, Industry and Competition
EE	-	Employment Equity
GCIS	-	Government Communication Information System
IEC	-	Independent Electoral Commission
ILO	-	International Labour Organisation
SABC	-	South African Broadcasting Corporation
SADC	-	Southern African Development Community
SAHRC	-	South African Human Rights Commission
SAPS	-	South African Police Service
StatsSA	-	Statistics South Africa
UN	-	United Nations

TERMS USED

Economic genocide is the deliberate bulk exclusion of persons from deserved economic opportunities and livelihoods.

Immigration is the international movement (arrival) of persons from one country into another.

Immigrant is a person who has moved from one country (normally country of birth or regular residence) to another country.

Irregular migration is migration which occurs outside of lawful requirements also known as illegal migration.

Migration is the general movement of persons from one place (of regular residence) to another.

Migrant is a person who moves from one place to another.

Migrant and Immigrant are primarily used interchangeably through the text to refer to foreign nationals, with very few instances where Internal Migrant is used to refer to SA citizens who migrate from province to province

TABLE OF CONTENTS

1. The New Democratic South Africa

1.1 Background

At the dawn of South Africa's (SA) democracy, black people young and old had high hopes to have their land and dignity restored after many years of repression at the hands of the colonial and apartheid ruling elite. This could play out in at least, one of two ways:

a) Continue with widespread revolts by citizens, underground military operations and international sanctions aimed at forcefully removing the colonisers from the land and repossessing all the profits derived therefrom or...

b) Have a negotiated peaceful transition, leading to the development of the *Constitution of the Republic of South Africa* (Constitution) *that would affirm all human dignity, equality, human rights, non-racialism and non-sexism for all South Africans* (South Africa, 1996).

South Africans chose the latter which was adopted by the United Nations (UN) as the *Declaration on Apartheid and its Destructive Consequences in Southern Africa,* on the 14 December 1989. This position was in fact initiated by the African National Congress (ANC) as the *Harare Declaration* through the Organisation of African Unity (OAU) on August 21, 1989 (UN, 1989). The Constitution's endorsement of the right to fair labour practices opened doors for black South Africans to obtain full exposure to work and business opportunities in humane conditions. This constitutional mandate led to the development of appropriate affirmative action legislation such as the *Employment Equity Act* (EE), the *Broad Based Black Economic Empowerment Act* (B-BBEE) and generally the *Labour Relations Act* (LRA). All these laws would then form the pillar of South Africa's peaceful transition into democracy in the early 90s. The existence of all the above-mentioned transformation and employment laws helped to create equitable conditions[1] which would ensure that black South African families get included as active beneficiaries in their own economy while the slow land reform process unfolded. Leaders of the liberation movements and the apartheid regime were hailed across the world as having done a sterling job in coming out with a Constitution that diffused a possible civil war between white and black people in South Africa (GCIS, 2016). The Constitution became the supreme law of the land and as many South Africans started to understand its contents, it then became the property of ordinary citizens. This implied that upholding constitutional prescripts was equal to implementing the desires and wishes of the general populace.

---

[1] South Africa (1998a). *Employment Equity Act 55 of 1998*

1.2 Transformation laws in SA

Transformation laws in South Africa were designed to include black South Africans into the country's mainstream economy to correct a previous imbalance that prioritised only white people. These laws also played an important role to appease the angry black South African whose immediate expectation was to get their land back from white settlers or go to war to achieve this. Such fears of disunity within the liberation movement were real as some were opposed to the idea of negotiating with the oppressive apartheid regime (Maharaj, 2008).

Given the size and impact of apartheid atrocities towards black South Africans, it can be accepted that the negotiated democratic peace settlement in SA amounted to a fairly good deal for white South Africans. That peaceful settlement came with an array of important immediate benefits for white citizens in South Africa as the new Constitution generally provided assurances that no black person would forcefully remove any white person from any land in the country to reverse apartheid land grabs. The Bill of Rights within the Constitution further prohibited any black person from attacking any white person and taking their material possessions to avenge apartheid social and economic crimes. Black South Africans were on the other hand persuaded to accept the new constitutional order which entrenched universal suffrage and the right to dignity for all citizens. The new democratic government was further understood to be committed to fully utilise the Constitution in developing relevant legislation to ensure that local black people who lost land due to colonial and apartheid land grabs, receive their land back within an organised legal framework. The state also undertook to equitably include local black people into their country's economy as meaningful participants through transformation legislation. Apart from the right to vote, transformation legislation and the continued implementation thereof may be the only tangible benefit (however little) that currently accrues to black people in the new democratic South Africa. This is the case because the lawful land re-distribution process is slow and further complicated by unpatriotic disagreements among those who are directly involved[2]. South Africa's transformation agenda was poised to get racial groups who were side-lined during apartheid to be afforded priority into the economy. The spirit and intent of all South Africa's transformation laws sought to prioritise the previously excluded communities without taking away the livelihoods of those who benefited during apartheid. This fact was captured vividly in the objectives of the *B-BBEE Act which sought to improve meaningful black participation and achieve substantial racial change in ownership within the economy*[3].

---

[2] Advisory Panel on Land Reform and Agriculture (2019). *Final report of the Advisory Panel on Land Reform and Agriculture.*
[3] South Africa (2003a). *B-BBEE Act 53 of 2003.*

1.3 The abuse of transformation laws in SA

The implementation of transformation laws in SA was prone to potential abuse and corruption. As aptly contended by Madi (2016), detractors of equity laws and civil society have become emboldened to question the significance of the actual benefits of transformation trickling down to a wider black participation. Some of the perceptions that arise in this regard include the following:

- ❖ Government empowerment contracts seen to be allocated to only those within some inner circle of influential leaders.
- ❖ The same people or entities seen to be getting empowerment deals in different sectors of the economy to the exclusion of many other deserving citizens.
- ❖ Black people seen to merely front their blackness in exchange for cash and not participate meaningfully to add value in empowerment roles.
- ❖ Business entities who front expats in transformation positions.

Transformation laws in South Africa when carefully read together with other legislation do offer full protection to all citizens, including white South Africans. The concept of demographic representation forms the bedrock of transformation laws in SA where the proportion of those occupying positions in the economy mimics the prevailing population demographics. This approach would fairly include all racial groups in South Africa's economic opportunities. *Section 8 of the Employment Services Act and Section 18 of the Immigration Regulations 2014 compel the economy to exhaust local skills before importing skills into SA.* For example, a corporation which appoints a black foreign executive with a rare qualification that no other local black person has, would still be in violation of the stated laws if there is a suitably qualified white South African to fill that position. The practice of creating a false distant impression of EE and B-BBEE compliance by importing black faces into prominent positions, while violating other sovereign laws should be rejected by all citizens. Political and business leaders would be abusing the country's transformation laws by telling their followers that such laws are anti-white. Given the spade of corruption in SA, the transformation agenda could be the only insulation between land repossession anarchy and peace. White politicians, who use deception and radicalism to bash transformation laws as mere reverse-racism, are just as irresponsible as black leaders who selfishly hog empowerment opportunities. This type of expedient and self-serving conduct by leaders poses a risk to the peace pact that holds South Africa's multiracial communities together.

Brazen rejection of transformation could also have necessitated the formation of black radical movements who justifiably become a credible voice for the landless and poor people in South Africa. The level of militancy within such organisations should also serve as a barometer on dwindling patience amongst the poor masses to share the real spoils of their democracy. These movements attract many descendants of apartheid victims, who were told at the dawn of democracy that things would be better if they offered their full forgiveness for all apartheid criminality and put their trust in the newly promulgated constitutional rights. It is common cause that when families do well economically/ financially, children get reasonable care through-out their upbringing to also become successful members of society.

Sefalafala (2020) also observed how unemployment presents problems beyond the lack of money by further exposing affected persons to stigma, low self-esteem, displacement and an overall sense of worthlessness. In essence joblessness does not only give rise to economic and physical hardship for affected families, it also pushes them into a painful psychological terrain. Families of the unemployed tend to face increased levels of conflict, tension and stress (Mandelbaum, 2019).

After hundreds of years of subjugation, black families in South Africa finally have an opportunity to do well through decent job and business opportunities enabled by transformation legislation. It is estimated that land reform efforts in SA have only managed to redistribute less than 10% of all commercial farmland into black hands in a period of 23 years since democracy (Advisory Panel on Land Reform and Agriculture, 2019). It would therefore be unwise to undermine and weaken transformation laws when many dispossessed people still cry out for land. All patriotic members of society should work together to improve black participation in the economy through transformation laws[4]. While it is reality that some transformation beneficiaries have through their reproachable conduct, managed to reduce empowerment to some kind of a swear word in business and social circles, all South Africans are cautioned to fix what is broken and avoid throwing the baby out with the bathwater. 'The country's peace and stability would be under constant threat for as long as black people feel excluded from meaningful economic activity' (Madi, 2016). Some of the senior political leaders in South Africa have managed to improve their lives and businesses through transformation laws. It is thus not too much to ask, for all empowerment beneficiaries to speak loudest in support for the strengthening of existing transformation legislation. Those who may take the power of forgiveness and reconciliation for granted are cautioned to remember the brutal execution of land-grabs by European despots who waged wars, spilling the blood of countless natives and subjecting many to years of servitude. It is logically difficult to forgive someone who does not recognise any wrongdoing on their part.

---

[4] DEL (2019). *Press Release: Labour court gives thumbs up to Employment Equity following court challenge.* Pretoria: DEL.

1.4 State abuse of transformation laws

The B-BBEE Commission's 2019 report on the national status and trends on transformation showed that 42% of JSE listed companies submitted their compliance reports compared with 15% of state organs. The low reporting by state organs is an irritation given that empowerment laws were developed to promote black participation in the economy by a black government. The report reflected overall compliance levels across various assessment categories ranging from 29% to 68% (DTIC, 2019). While the numbers are still too low for comfort, there is a positive hint that some entities are trying to comply with existing laws to transform. The state on the other hand is observably leading by bad example in their uninspired response in the submission of compliance reports and this presents opportunity for detractors of transformation to keep bashing these efforts. To create laws and silently abandon them after a few black elites have benefited is a betrayal of black people by black leaders.

It would eventually become intolerable for the ruling class to repeatedly engage in the brazen abuse of transformation efforts and scapegoat colonialism and apartheid whenever citizens demand accountability. The practice of attacking the accuser by politicians faced with criticism or caught on the wrong side the law to deflect attention, is an abhorrent phenomenon which is getting much needed exposure and should be avoided in SA (Smudde and Courtright 2008). All black and white political leaders have a joint responsibility to honour the political sacrifice that the majority of ordinary South Africans made to lay the peaceful foundation to the democratic state. Divisive rhetoric by leaders should be avoided as it may incite hostile stereotypes among communities. Our constitutional peaceful democracy is supported by the three main pillars of lawful land redistribution, transformation laws and moral leadership, all of which are incubated within the fragile power of forgiveness. We are therefore collectively responsible to make sure that this centre holds!

1.5 Transformation in African countries

Transformation in South Africa is not a unique intervention as there are many African countries who after gaining independence, embarked on transformation drives to recalibrate the means of access to opportunities for previously denied local communities.

In their lament over the slow pace of equity in workplaces, the Commission for Employment Equity (CEE) in South Africa highlighted some of the adverse findings in their 2019/20 annual report. The CEE pointed to the employment of foreign nationals in top management positions as well as their increasing presence in entry level occupations, despite existing laws restricting such appointments (CEE, 2020). South Africans seem to have respected other sovereign states by not availing themselves to occupy key transformation positions in any independent country. It is therefore important to interrogate the phenomenon that many expatriates occupy transformation positions both in government service and private industry.

As expressed by Mbeki (2016), South Africa was always committed to respect the right of sovereign states to determine their future. This stance was also adamantly opposed to any foreign imposition of solutions upon any sovereign state, a position which is perfectly aligned with several laws of the African Union (AU).

- ❖ *Article 3(b) of the Constitutive Act of the AU affirms the commitment of the Union to defend the sovereignty, territorial integrity and independence of its member states.*
- ❖ *Article 4(a) endorses the principle of sovereign equality and interdependence among member states of the Union.*
- ❖ *Article 4(b) calls for member states to respect borders existing on achievement of independence.*
- ❖ *Article 4(g) prohibits interference by any member state in the internal affairs of another.*
- ❖ *Article 3, Sections (1) and (2) of the AU Protocol on free movement in the continent, declares that cross border movements should be based on the respect for laws and policies of the host state as well as transparency* (AU, 2018).

South Africa as a sovereign state must transparently provide reasons to her citizens for the rising number of non-nationals in empowerment positions, in seeming violation of local laws and AU treaties. Sometimes all it would take to diffuse tensions could be just transparency as called for by the AU. This is critical in the context of the intended unity of the continent to prevent hatred brewing among locals towards expats who could be seen as taking undeserved sovereign opportunities in SA.

1.5.1 *The Constitution of Zimbabwe*

The constitution of Zimbabwe unashamedly prioritises Zimbabwean nationals in the economy and empowerment opportunities in that country.

❖ *Section 12(1)(a) of the Constitution of Zimbabwe Amendment Act 20 of 2013 states that Zimbabwe's foreign policy must be based on principles that include the promotion and protection of the national interests of Zimbabwe.*

❖ *Section 13(1)(c) affirms that the state of Zimbabwe must strive to facilitate rapid and equitable development of industrial and commercial enterprises to empower Zimbabwean citizens.*

❖ *Section 14(1) instructs the Zimbabwean state to take measures to empower all marginalised persons and communities in Zimbabwe through appropriate, transparent, fair and just affirmative action.*

❖ *Section 14(2) compels the state of Zimbabwe to take adequate measures to create employment for all Zimbabweans, especially* women and the youth.

* Section 20(1)(c) instructs the Zimbabwean state at all levels, to take reasonable measures including affirmative action programmes to ensure that the youth aged between 15 and 35 years, are afforded opportunities for employment and other avenues to economic empowerment (Zimbabwe, 2013).

* Zimbabwe's Indigenisation and Economic Empowerment Act 14 of 2007 was designed to support measures for the economic empowerment of indigenous Zimbabweans. Section 3(1)(a) of this act stipulated that at least 51% of the shares of every public company and any other business shall be owned by indigenous Zimbabweans (Zimbabwe, 2007).

1.5.2 The Constitution of Nigeria

The Constitution of Nigeria prioritises Nigerian citizens.

* Section 16(1)(a) of the Constitution of the Federal Republic of Nigeria affirms the state commitment to harness the resources of the nation and promote national prosperity and an efficient, dynamic and self-reliant economy.

* Section 16(2)(d) says that the State shall direct its policy towards ensuring that suitable and adequate shelter, suitable and adequate food, reasonable national minimum living wage, old age care and pensions, and unemployment, sick benefits and welfare of the disabled are provided for all citizens.

- ❖ Section 17(3)(a) says that the State shall direct its policy towards ensuring all citizens, without discrimination on any group whatsoever, have the opportunity for securing adequate means of livelihood as well as adequate opportunity to secure suitable employment.
- ❖ Section 19(a) determines the first foreign policy objective of Nigeria as the promotion and protection of the national interest (Nigeria, 1999).
- ❖ The Nigerian President issued a directive barring the employment of immigrants in jobs that Nigerians can do, also compelling the state to prioritise local companies (Buhari, 2018).

1.5.3   The Constitution of Malawi

The Constitution of Malawi prioritises citizens of Malawi.

- ❖ Section 12(i) stipulates that all legal and political authority of the State derives from the people of Malawi and shall be exercised in accordance with this Constitution solely to serve and protect their interests.
- ❖ Section 13(n) stipulates that the State shall actively promote the welfare and development of the people of Malawi by progressively adopting and implementing policies and legislation aimed at achieving economic management. This is to be achieved through a sensible balance between the creation

and distribution of wealth through the nurturing of a market economy and long-term investment in health, education, economic and social development programmes.

❖ *Section 30(2) stipulates that the State shall take all necessary measures for the realization of the right to development. Such measures shall include, amongst other things, equality of opportunity for all in their access to basic resources, education, health services, food, shelter, employment and infrastructure* (Malawi, 1997).

❖ *One of the functions of the Department of Immigration in Malawi is stated as monitoring, tracking, apprehending, deporting and repatriating illegal immigrants in order to promote security of the country and safeguard jobs for natives* (Malawi, Government).

1.6 Summarising comments

South Africa's rainbow democracy is pillared on lawful land reform and transformation to include many previously excluded citizens into the economy. The country's inclusive democracy can be rekindled through a commitment by all black and white leaders:

➜ To embrace transformation as the key component of the peaceful contract in South Africa's democracy and not just an option for some to abuse and reject at will.

➜ To avoid replacing local transformation beneficiaries with expatriates as this could be seen as brazen betrayal of local citizens by employers and expats who accept such positions causing possible tensions locally and continentally.

➔ To be responsible in their political rhetoric on transformation as it impacts on the racial harmony within communities.

➔ To unite in calling upon the state to lead by example in complying with existing transformation laws.

2. The Influx of Cheap Labour into SA

2.1 Cheap labour explained

Cheap labour is described as the availability of people willing to work in lower than widely accepted lawful labour conditions. In many instances the cheap labourer would offer their services in return for anything ranging from food to accommodation and low wages in desperation to survive. It is also reasonable to expect that the cheap labourer knows that by offering the cheapest services they would undercut the normal jobseeker. In other words, the activities of the cheap labourer are also possibly driven by deliberate intentions to be the preferred employee (Fevre, 1984). The desire to secure livelihoods pushes human beings to move from saturated environments to other hopeful spaces. This phenomenon is called migration or immigration when it specifically relates to international movements. Many countries of the world have specific legislation to regulate immigration in a bid to protect limited resources for their citizens. Such immigration laws[5] would generally be friendly to immigrants who bring specialised or scarce skills into a country. However, people who come into a country to find jobs in non-specialised areas are prohibited or highly restricted in the numbers allowed because host citizens would deserve priority into such non-specialised jobs (South Africa, 2002). The rampant influx of cheap

---

[5] South Africa (2002). *Immigration Act 13 of 2002.*

labour into any country could have severe economic consequences for citizens as many in the job market could be effectively replaced by cheap labourers. This possibility exists because businesses in a capitalist economy tend to cherish efforts aimed at reducing operational costs and specifically, labour costs. While labour market regulation affects the conduct of businesses in selecting employees to remain profitable, such interventions are primarily aimed at protecting the most vulnerable stakeholders in job transactions (Butschek; Sauerman, 2019). The insatiable desire to amass wealth by exploiting the poverty and desperation of others has existed for thousands of years commonly known as greed. The notion that cheap labour serves a role to neutralise rising wages that become unaffordable for employers, may just be a ploy to use slavery for greed-centred outcomes. This posture mainly comes from market deregulation gangs who wish away the existence of labour laws, worker rights and unions from any economy. The advent of globalisation has called for labour market flexibility within countries interested in attracting transnational investments. This development has unfortunately contributed to the amelioration of greater preferences for cheap labour leading to fractured social cohesion between foreign labourers and local communities (Mihaly, 2015). The reality that cheap labourers (many of whom happen to be immigrants) suffer greater abuses in jobs they occupy, presents a risk because there is a limit to the amount of suffering that a human being can endure (Masterman-Smith; Elton, 2007). One could argue that the solution to an employer's inability to afford paying fair wages for labour simply lies in transparency. Big businesses including medium enterprises are notorious for their refusal to pay fair wages to workers when individual executives would take home millions in salaries, bonuses and perks. Logically if employers would openly share their financials with workers, then all stakeholders would be appropriately informed in the game of affordability. Labour unions would not unreasonably pitch unaffordable demands if actual profits were transparently discussed with workers. The veil of secrecy surrounding company profits is likely driven by greed, where a few high-ranking individuals share massive profits to the exclusion of workers. The deliberate attraction of cheap migrant labour to gain access to fresh talent would be grossly misplaced if the prevailing job market conditions are not factored into such decisions. In the context of Africa, such interventions if not well considered have the potential to fracture continental unity efforts as the rising displacement of local jobseekers would likely lead to hostilities. The phenomenon that immigrants tend to be absorbed in non-specialised areas, poses a further continental dilemma of wasting the same fresh talent on precarious work (Brown; Danson, 2008).

2.2 The negative impact of cheap labour in SA

As noted in their response to the Syrian refugee crisis in Jordan, the ILO (2019) observed that the refugee influx exerted downward pressure on wages in Jordan's labour market, increased child labour as well as displaced low-skilled workers in that country. Similarly, the uncontrolled rise in the number of cheap labourers coming into South Africa from other countries has the propensity to constrict an already saturated job market as well as keep local people out of jobs. This risk gets more pronounced due to the scanty availability of immigration reports to guide government leaders on the actual numbers of people entering South Africa.

Statistics South Africa (StatsSA) is the official research and data collection agency in this country mandated to provide political heads and decision makers with reliable reports on population dynamics and migration patterns.

The statistical agency released a hard-hitting report on migration in South Africa called the 'Labour Market Outcomes of Migrant Populations in South Africa between 2012 and 2017'. In this report StatsSA (2019) showed that more than 1.25 million jobs were in the hands of immigrants in South Africa in 2017. In other words, over 1.25 million jobs were held by foreign nationals while there were 5.9 million South Africans who desperately needed these jobs in their own country. The report further reflected the unemployment rate of foreign nationals in South Africa to be 18.4% compared with 26.7% for locals back in 2017 (StatsSA, 2018). This research also found that foreign nationals were almost 2 times more likely to get jobs in South Africa than locals.

The usual allegation that immigrants get offered many non-scarce jobs in South Africa is therefore substantiated as empirically evidenced in this report. This report was sadly, silently kept in the hands of the state President even in the heat of violence between unemployed locals and foreign employees.

Ordinary South Africans continue to observe helplessly, the increasing employment of foreign nationals in simple jobs that many unemployed locals can occupy such as cashiers at retail stores, general workers, admin workers at car dealerships, sales representatives, construction workers, waiters at restaurants, truck drivers, cleaners/ domestic workers, television presenters, camera operators, news field staff, and the list goes on.

The informal economy in South Africa located in the rural areas, townships and cities was also showing the informal employment of immigrants to be 29% in this sector compared to locals at 17%. This situation was doomed to explode at some point as many unemployed South Africans got side-lined in their own job market. StatsSA (2019) importantly indicated the 5-year growth rate of the working age population[6] between 2012 and 2017 to have been extremely high

---

[6] Working age population refers to those aged between 15 and 64 years.

(49%) for immigrants in South Africa compared to SA citizens at no more than 16%.

The prescripts of pan-Africanism appeal to all Africans to work together in solving African problems[7]. The ideology and practice of pan-Africanism seek to forge a united Africa which would be leveraged for the collective bail-out of distressed Africans by those with enough resources to share. Judging by the numbers shared by StatsSA above, what we currently observe in South Africa is not pan-Africanism but a dangerous misappropriation of one country's resources possibly for selfish gain by individuals.

2.3 Work visa laws in SA

While South Africa's leaders appear too eager to please their counterparts in the continent at the expense of existing laws, statistical evidence shows that these leaders are not true to the pan-African agenda. If there was genuine love for Africans, leaders would put a stop to the enslavement of African migrants in the local job market as official reports confirm such slave conditions (see section 2.6). Political power should be used to ensure that when migrants enter South Africa, they do so legally to enjoy many privileges as all locals do. This means creating a climate where compliance to immigration laws would lead to regular and safe migration in line with country commitments to the United Nations

---

[7] Malisa, M; Nhengeze, P. (2018). Pan-Africanism: A quest for liberation and the pursuit of a united Africa. *Genealogy, 2(3), p. 28.*

Sustainable Development Goals (SDGs).

On the other hand, to use political power to issue work visas for non-scarce skills, in contravention of the *Immigration Act* would be the same as entrenching the harm caused by cheap labour on local jobseekers leading to hatred towards immigrants. Such conduct would be a further endorsement of the slave conditions that immigrants are exposed to.

The *Immigration Act 13 of 2002* is the main legislative instrument that provides guidelines for accepted conduct by all who enter and leave South Africa. It is supported by various other sovereign laws with the aim of ensuring harmonious coexistence among citizens and those who visit or wish to live in the country. Such migration laws are not unique to South Africa as various countries across the world have similar legislation to regulate the in and out movement of people. These laws ensure the legal availability of visa options for those who choose to visit, study, work or do business in a foreign country. It is also important to mention that immigration and other laws seek to uphold the safety and security of both natives and visitors. The mandate to ensure that all who enter a country get properly documented is key in holding all residents accountable when necessary.

Section 18(3)(a) of the Immigration Regulations 2014 states that an application for a general work visa should be accompanied by a certificate from the Department of Labour confirming that:

i. despite diligent search, the prospective employer has been unable to find a suitably skilled and qualified South African or permanent resident to fill the vacancy.

ii. The applicant is qualified/ proven skills aligned to job offer.

iii. the job conditions and remuneration are not inferior to those prevailing in that market segment for citizens or permanent residents.

Paragraph (i) of this section of the Regulations seeks to make it almost impossible for any employer to allow thousands of general workers from outside of SA when there are millions of unemployed citizens who can fill those positions. The emphasis is on 'critical skills' not readily available locally.

Paragraph (iii) pre-empts the scourge of cheap, slave labour practices. SA laws are in this case, seen to have full regard for the labour rights of immigrants. The big flop is that many expected that political leaders would be keen to uphold these laws to protect both immigrants and locals.

It is reasonable to expect the Department of Home Affairs (DHA) to factor in the prevailing industry and labour market indicators such as jobless rates before making decisions to issue general work visas. This may help to avoid specific markets from being disrupted by disgruntled unemployed locals. Without such labour market clarity, issued visas might affect job sectors and social cohesion adversely. For example, if the prevailing local unemployment rates are too high then any reasonable decision maker would strongly reject all attempts to issue such visas as that would effectively put a further strain on a job market that is already not able to provide jobs to millions of its unemployed citizens.

It is in the best interest of state leaders to ensure that South Africa's industries are not negatively impacted by the issuing of work visas. When the trucking industry faces an onslaught from angry local unemployed truck drivers protesting and burning trucks of employers who hire foreign visa holders, then issuing such work visas becomes the perfect recipe for that industrial disaster. A sensible leader would be expected to stop the issuing of work visas if the local construction industry would face angry unemployed citizens carrying guns to demand inclusion into their construction sector that is seen to be hiring foreign visa holders to the exclusion of locals.

South Africa's labour market is increasingly looking like a war zone, where political leaders watch from a distance when immigrants and locals clash for jobs. The battle-field conditions are steadily created when politicians make decisions that flout existing laws and the obvious dictates of local market conditions and empirical reports.

Section 8(2)(a) of the Employment Services Act of SA is aligned with the *Immigration Regulations 2014* in warning against employing foreign nationals in jobs that South Africans can occupy.

2.4 Displacing local graduates

The importation of the so-called critical skills into South Africa could also be abused to further push locals out of jobs and career opportunities. To employ a graduate from another country when there are thousands of unemployed graduates locally still seems to violate the *Immigration Regulations 2014* and other laws. It would also be a gross violation of the human rights of young South African graduates to prioritise foreign graduates in local jobs.

'Non-scarce skill' jobs are not only the unprofessional or low paying type. A qualified teacher or lecturer from another country for example, would still be bringing non-scarce skills into SA if there are already many unemployed citizens suitably qualified to teach. Employing a foreign national with a doctorate as a professor in any field if there are hundreds of suitably qualified South Africans would still amount to importing non-scarce skills in seeming violation of the country's laws. A state that allows its skilled and professional human capital base to be systematically overlooked in job opportunities would simply be sowing the seed of hatred towards expatriates. Even if a state was to be moved by compassion and humanitarian instincts against better judgement to share a strained job market like South Africa, it should reasonably not include issuing thousands of work visas, let alone millions.

Despite empirical evidence warning against the decision to issue general work visas, leaders seem to continue violating local job seekers consequently plunging local families into abject poverty and creating fertile conditions for hatred towards immigrants.

Table 1: Education status of those who migrated within 5 years of the survey date				
	Internal migrant (SA)		Immigrant (Foreigner)	
	(2007-2012)	(2012-2017)	(2007-2012)	(2012-2017)
Tertiary	21,6%	18,6%	13,2%	10,3%
SecondaryCompleted	30,4%	35,7%	26,6%	16,8%
SecondaryNotCompleted	38,7%	37,9%	44%	52,3%
PrimaryCompleted	2,7%	2%	4,8%	5,9%
LessThanPrimaryCompleted	5,2%	4,5%	7,1%	12%
No schooling	1,4%	1,3%	4,3%	2,8%

Source: Statistics South Africa

Table 1 above shows an analysis of the education status of persons who migrated within 5 years of the date when the survey was conducted. Such a phenomenon is also known as period migration. Internal-migrants are South Africans who were enumerated (surveyed) in a different province from province of origin.

The table shows that between 2007 and 2012, about 21.6% of SA Internal-migrants had tertiary qualifications compared to 13.2% of Immigrants. The same is also true for the time between 2012 and 2017, where 18.6% of South Africans had tertiary qualifications versus only 10.3% of Immigrants. It is also notable that the proportion of locals who did not complete secondary education decreased from 38.7% to 37.9% between the periods (2007-2012) and (2012-2017), while the proportion of immigrants who entered SA without matric increased from 44% to 52.3% during the same period. Contrary to popular believe that South Africans are less schooled than foreign nationals, the evidence depicted in the entire table shows that locals are significantly more educated than immigrants who came into the country during the period under review. In essence Table 1 shows how SA has been attracting many immigrants into the job market who are evidently less educated than locally available skills. The stage seems to be forcefully set for the systematic displacement of local jobseekers. If this phenomenon is not immediately halted, it could lead to the overall economic genocide of South Africans prompting an all-out protest against immigrants in general.

2.5 Unemployment and gender-based violence (GBV)

It is common cause that women who remain in abusive relationships do so for economic reasons sometimes. A woman, who is without a job or any income to sustain herself away from an abusive provider, would be stuck in such a relationship for survival. This translates to say that the employment of women in meaningful jobs is a step in the right direction to curb gender-based violence (Monakali et al, 2011). This would effectively afford the abused woman the confidence to leave the relationship and still be able to provide for herself and her children. In their final quarter of the 2017 Quarterly Labour Force Survey, StatsSA (2018) revealed that of the 5.9 million unemployed South Africans in that year, 2.9 million were women. We have already shown in the previous chapters that more than 1.25 million jobs were swallowed by foreign nationals in that same year. It was also shown that immigrants were 2 times more advantaged to occupy South African jobs than locals (StatsSA, 2019).

We should not cease to wonder whether the Presidency is doing something or nothing about the contribution of uncontrolled immigration on the jobs bloodbath in South Africa as shown in the official reports. What we know for certain, is that while something is being done or nothing at all, the devastating trends of cheap foreign labour persist, and are possibly getting worse.

By not taking decisive action on these immigration matters, the Presidency opens room for that highest office in the land to be lambasted for:

❖ The bad politics in making more than 2.9 million South African women jobseekers to wait while more than 1.25 million existing jobs get handed over to foreign nationals.
❖ The irresponsibility to prioritise the poverty of foreign nationals over the poverty of local women jobseekers in their own country.
❖ The hypocrisy to speak of creating millions of jobs when the

stage has been set for the local job market to replace South African workers with cheap foreign labourers.

❖ The deception to send hollow messages of support to the suffering of South African women when millions of unemployed SA women get overlooked for jobs in favour of female foreign workers.

❖ Taking job opportunities away from South African nationals which breeds hatred towards all foreign nationals leading to violence where women (local & foreign) suffer the most.

Some of the millions of unemployed South Africans are ordinary branch members of the ruling party. This means, the prioritisation of foreign women in South African jobs affects members of the ruling party and the general society in equal harsh measure. A president is like a father to the entire nation. It is cruelty for a father to prioritise the poverty of a neighbour's neglected children by taking away the little food from the mouths of his own children.

2.6 Slave conditions of cheap labour in SA

It is sad that the slavery of poor Africans remains a practice that has survived for centuries and is still currently enjoyed by those in positions of political and economic power.

The International Labour Organisation (ILO) defines decent work as opportunities for work that is productive and delivers a fair income, security in the workplace and social protection for families, better prospects for personal development and social integration, freedom for people to express their concerns, organize and participate in the decisions that affect their lives and equality of opportunity and treatment for all women and men.

Table 2: Decent Work Agenda Analysis in SA (2017)			
	SA non-movers (Province bound)	SA internal-migrant (Provincial mover)	Immigrants (Foreigner)
Unemployment rate	29,1%	25,8%	**18,4%**
NEET rate (15-24)	29,6%	34,2%	**37,7%**
Informal employment	17,4%	13,7%	**29,3%**
% work excessive hours	27,1%	27,5%	**39,1%**
% qualify maternity	57,4%	65,7%	**44,6%**
% with job contract	81,2%	83,1%	**59,5%**
% in permanent jobs	60,9%	67,2%	**49,9%**
% with pension	47,9%	56,5%	**32,5%**
% with UIF	59,7%	67,9%	**44,4%**
% union membership	29,7%	33,1%	**15,7%**

Source: Statistics South Africa

The 'SA non-mover' column in the above table refers to South African citizens who were enumerated (surveyed) in their province of origin, while the 'SA Internal migrants' column deals with local citizens who were enumerated in a different province from their province of birth. This table shows how immigrants who occupy jobs in South Africa are treated much worse than locals. The proportion of foreign nationals who are subjected to working excessive hours is highest at **39.1%** compared to locals at 27.5% and below. The percentage of foreign nationals who qualify for maternity/ paternity leave in SA jobs is lowest **(44.6%)** compared with 65.7% and 57.4% of SA migrants and SA non-movers respectively. The proportion of foreign nationals who have an employment contract was lowest at **59.5%** compared to 83.1% and 81.2% of SA internal migrants and SA non-movers respectively. The proportion of foreign nationals in permanent jobs is lowest **(49.9%)**, those with employer contribution to pension **(32.5%)** and unemployment insurance fund UIF **(44.4%)** are fewest compared to SA nationals. Foreign nationals with union membership are lowest at **15.7%** compared to SA nationals.

In summary the table shows that foreign nationals in South Africa's jobs suffer greater labour abuses than locals.

The low unemployment rate of foreigners **(18.4%)** in SA suggests that they get prioritised in jobs because they may be more susceptible to slave working conditions. When left unhindered, the proliferation of unfair labour practices has the undesirable propensity to normalise modern day slavery. *Article 4 of the Universal Declaration of Human Rights* (UDHR) *prohibits slavery, servitude and slave trade in all its forms. Section 13 of the Constitution of SA also prohibits slavery, servitude and forced* *labour.* Legislative enforcement should therefore be sufficiently focused to prevent the existence of any form of slavery. *Section 18(3)(a) of the Immigration Regulations 2014 seeks to pre-empt slave labour practices by compelling employers to afford immigrants the same conditions of employment applicable to citizens.*

It is also undeniable that the above table highlights significant incapacity in the enforcement of existing labour laws, failing to even protect employed South African citizens. The table shows significant numbers of employed locals also bearing the brunt of unlawful labour practices leading to slave conditions. It would have been prudent for South Africa as a new democratic state to first improve the employment conditions of her citizens before allowing millions of immigrants to enter an already lawless and saturated labour market. This country has an array of good laws that if enforced consistently and exhaustively can protect citizens and immigrants from job related abuses and clashes.

Slave labour involves a mix of other crimes like human and child trafficking. This possibility exists because entities that prefer cheap labour may expect a steady pipeline supply of the required human slave capital to maintain their illicit super-profit objectives[8]. Any country that is serious about combating the scourge of human

---

[8] DEL (2020). *Media statement: JHB magistrates court to hear the application for leave to appeal the bail in the Chinese human trafficking and violation of SA labour laws case.* Pretoria: DEL

trafficking and slavery must first look into strengthening and optimally enforcing existing immigration and labour laws. *Goal 8.7 of the United Nation's SDGs enjoins all countries of the world to institute immediate and effective measures to eradicate modern slavery and human trafficking.*

All the evidence exposed in this section demonstrated the harsh effects of uncontrolled immigration on both South African citizens and foreign nationals. The Presidency receives all the official statistical reports to enable sound policy decisions to protect the sovereignty of the country and the livelihoods of citizens. Cabinet ministers, who forcefully issue general work visas against the obvious dictates of the South African job market conditions and existing laws, are responsible for violations of the rights of citizens. When citizens get dehumanised, they could start directing their anger towards foreign nationals causing scores of immigrants in SA to live in fear. It is however a sitting president who appoints cabinet members and therefore their activities must follow the law of the land as championed by the President himself.

Getting wealthy through the blood and sweat of others without fair compensation is un-Godly conduct in any language or religion. Those businesses who engage in unfair labour practices are thus inviting a curse upon their heads and might as well kiss lady prosperity good-bye. 'Look, the wages you failed to pay the workers who mowed your fields are crying out against you. The cries of the harvesters have reached the ears of the Lord Almighty.'[9] The NEET rate in the above table refers to young people between the ages of 15 and 24 years who are not employed, not in educational institutions, and not in any form of training. In simple terms these are young potential job market entrants in South Africa. The proportion of immigrants in this category is highest at 37.7% compared to locals at no more than 34.2%. This should raise concern among all residents to have many youngsters who find themselves in a foreign country without support or family backup that may be available to local youngsters in a similar situation (Pratt, 2020). The fact that jobs are not available even for millions of South Africans, raises the question of how jobless foreign nationals survive without basic human needs such as food.

2.7 The enslavement of rare-skilled expats

There is a case to be made about foreign nationals in powerful rare-skill positions and the kind of pressures they get subjected to. Legal frameworks may contribute to a misdiagnosis of existing slave conditions due to stereotypes associated with foreign nationals where many get lawfully probed on immigration and other criminality without investigating willful participation to expose coercion or trafficking (Ramiz et al., 2020). Anecdotally, there is a tendency to expect instant loyalty from an expat whereas a local

---

[9] Biblica Inc. (2011). *Holy Bible: New International Version: James 5:4.*

incumbent of an influential position would be appropriately lobbied to pledge their loyalty on any subject matter. This unreasonable expectation on the foreigner should also be seen as part of the emotional enslavement of rare-skilled expats in prominent positions. People who move to other countries for various reasons are subjected to stress related to adaptation to new environments also known as acculturation. Generally, the host country would expect immigrants to embrace prevailing dominant cultures to fit in among local communities. Mono-ethnic environments tend to present greater challenges for expats to be accepted and made to feel welcome compared to multi-ethnic countries where the degree of tolerance for mixed cultures among residents is higher (Steinmetz, 2013). It would however be difficult to compile an overwhelming account on the emotional enslavement of expats in powerful positions because the positions are for powerful people who should never cry. In South Africa where black professionals are seen as profit cows for industries that seek to fulfill the country's empowerment requirements, expats can potentially be abused to front their blackness or rare-skill without any real intention by the employer to fully utilise their abilities. Unlike the poor and un-certificated foreigner, society expects the rare-skilled expat to be sufficiently capacitated to negotiate fair outcomes through complex interactions with an employer. The reality however, is that when one is far away from home and desperate to earn a living, human beings tend to be less demanding of market related conditions to avoid any stalemate that could prevent entry into a job or sustainability within an occupation. In their study on the psychosocial experiences of African migrants in Germany, France, Italy, the Netherlands, and the UK, Idemudia and Boehnke (2020) found that migration related stress negatively affected the mental health of migrants. If the plight of foreign nationals with scarce skills is not identified and addressed, then a host country may not derive the optimal benefit to grow the economy from such skills. It is therefore critical to be mindful of the various nuanced pressures facing expats. They are valued guests to be treated fairly, as human beings within the economy and society in general. Rare skilled expats together with all documented foreign nationals are invited to join local communities in discouraging irregular migration. This would enhance solidarity with host country citizens to undermine generalised negative perceptions towards immigrants. Progressive countries of the world have introduced labour laws that are geared to combat slavery or practices that resemble slavery. Many are also becoming increasingly aware of modern-day slavery as a system that denies workers basic labour rights such as reasonable wages and humane working conditions.

2.8 Summarising comments

Any state which intends to economically genocide their citizens should look no further than the following algorithm currently loading in South Africa:

→ Violate existing immigration and labour laws to issue thousands of work-visas to flood a job market with cheap foreign labour.

→ Create a 'pull-factor' by allowing massive entry of less educated immigrants to replace citizens in jobs.

→ Allow a 5-year growth of working age population of immigrants to be more than 3 times (49%) that of locals (16%).

→ Allow rampant non-compliance to labour and immigration laws to pave the way for abusive slave labour practices.

→ Create a job market which absorbs immigrants at almost 2 times the likelihood for locals.

→ Accept a low jobless rate (18.4%) for immigrants compared to that for local citizens (26.7%).

→ Enable lawless conditions for the local informal economy to be dominated by immigrants at 29% versus local citizens at 17%.

→ Ignore all existing laws and scramble to create instant 'unlawful' provisions to legalise the status quo.

→ Dismiss all complaints by citizens as baseless and do nothing as a state.

3. Prioritisation of Citizens

3.1 Prioritisation of citizens in African states

While South Africans are unhappy with their leaders for allowing irregular migration to push citizens out of their own economy, there are African leaders who unwaveringly put their citizens' interests above all others.

The Nigerian President issued an Executive Order in 2018 prohibiting foreign nationals from getting visas for jobs that Nigerian citizens can do. This order also compelled state institutions to prioritise Nigerian companies in the awarding of state contracts (Buhari, 2018). Nigerian leaders further closed the Nigerian inland borders towards the end of 2019 to curb the smuggling of food products, the influx of arms and hard drugs into Nigeria. The Nigerian President through the official government press release further mentioned that 'he could not stand by and watch the Nigerian youth getting destroyed by the influx of cheap hard drugs and arms into his country' (Adesina, 2020).

Public affirmations and enforcement of sovereign laws governing migration by leaders should be the preferred proactive measure to curb irregular migration as opposed to deportation which is harsh for those affected.

Political decision makers in Angola expelled more than 300 000 illegal migrants in 2018. This they reportedly did to restructure and protect their mining economy and citizens from the rampant diamond smuggling in that country. It is undeniable that when so many migrants have to leave a country within a stipulated short time frame, there would be chaos which would open doors for human rights abuses. The United Nations issued an alert regarding the humanitarian plight of the affected migrants also pleading with the state of Angola to slow down the pace of further deportations (UN, 2018). While it is reasonable to have wished for a staggered deportation to smoothen the departure of thousands of migrants, it is also possible that the Angolan government were pressured by their own sovereign needs which they duly had to prioritise. Sovereign states reserve the right to enforce laws that allow or refuse entry through their borders (Long et al, 2011). The accumulation of a large number of irregular migrants could be a symptom of widespread non-compliance to immigration and other sovereign laws. The United Nation's SDGs sought the commitment of all countries to facilitate the safe and orderly movement of people between countries through appropriate legislation (UN, 2015). This implies that nations of the world are expected to implement existing laws to prevent the cumulative effects of irregular migration which eventually necessitate mass deportations from affected countries.

Zambian authorities issued a statement in 2018, giving effect to the expulsion of foreign nationals trading illegally within that country. In a strong worded statement from the Ministry of Home Affairs in Zambia, illegal foreign traders were warned to 'leave the country on their own accord as Zambian authorities would no longer condone their illegal activities.' The statement further declared that Zambian nationals who rent out trading spaces to illegal foreign nationals would be dealt with in accordance with the laws of that country. The Ministry also appealed to all law-abiding citizens of Zambia to report any person violating laws and those trading in undesignated spaces, to law enforcement agencies (Zambia Ministry of Home Affairs, 2018).

The spread of covid-19 across the globe has prompted many leaders, including many African leaders to reserve jobs, opportunities and limited resources for their citizens. This is because even some of the strongest economies of the world were adversely impacted by the spread of this virus. South Africa's leaders seem to be the only ones who are not prepared to make declarations on prioritising citizens on jobs and services due to depleted resources further aggravated by covid-19.

3.2 Desperation to silence SA citizens & leaders

South African leaders have expressed opinions and cautionary sentiments on migration in the recent past. A former Deputy

Minister of Police was sharply silenced for his remarks on the growing high number of foreign nationals in Johannesburg (SAPS 2018). The Deputy Minister was well within his right to question the high number of visitors in his backyard. We often make the mistake of thinking that a serving minister speaks for himself, when his voice of reason should represent millions of citizens who elect a government. In 2019 South Africans saw foreign traders attacking the country's law enforcement officers with objects, bricks and petrol bombs when the police tried to conduct mandated operations. That attack was characterised as an attempt by foreign criminals to co-govern and turn South Africa into a criminal enclave (SAPS, 2019c). Strangely, no human rights body spoke about the possible psychological trauma and rage among citizens at seeing their protectors and sovereignty being trampled upon in broad day light. True pan-Africanism does not require a single African state to host citizens from other countries without careful considerations for policing and security resources.

A former Minister of Health observed that many children born in local hospitals belonged to non-citizens. The Minister had on several occasions correctly pointed to shortcomings within the local health sector in meeting the constitutional rights of citizens to adequate healthcare[10]. In other words, South Africa cannot provide sufficient

---

[10] SABC (2018). *News article: Foreign nationals are burdening the SA health system: Motsoaledi*

health services to her citizens and logically that means any foreign national coming into the country would add to this severity. The Minister's observations and utterances in relation to migration were not unique as the ILO (2019) had already expressed a similar opinion. In their comment on the influx of Syrian refugees into Jordan, the labour body warned of the added pressures faced by Jordan's infrastructure and resources. To vilify a serving Minister for speaking out on matters which are in the public domain is a recipe for irritation among host country citizens. *Article 3(2)(b) of the AU protocol for the treaty on the free movement of persons in the continent affirms that such movements should be based on respect for laws and policies on the protection of national security, public order, public health, the environment and from any other factors that would be detrimental to the host state* (AU, 2018). As citizens, we should encourage the kind of leadership that shows capability in appropriately diagnosing services required relative to numbers of recipients. Civil rights groups in South Africa put a lot of pressure on politicians for the noble purpose of upholding the prescripts of democratic accountability. While the role of these entities is commendable, it also comes with potential harm if the rights of immigrants get elevated far above the rights of citizens. Lobby groups who for example, loudly decry the bad status of SA health facilities and conveniently omit to question the crashing effects of irregular migration on the same facilities risk being seen as noncaring for local citizens. This kind of selective oversight is a betrayal of citizens' rights. International lobby and humanitarian entities are known for providing some of the best career paths for their staff working in other countries, thus attracting a class of aspiring scholars into humanitarian work. Such career perks could inspire apathy to underplay the real plight of migrants and host country communities to keep humanitarian missions relevant and funded (Farah, 2020). A typical state also has a fair share of big corporations with huge resources who can potentially fund lobbyists to effect law regime changes for selfish profit agendas. It is also fair to expect the state to be strong enough to thwart unreasonable pressure from lobby groups. Citizens should however also demand accountability from lobbyists for the weakening of the legislative fabric meant to protect citizens. It is not pan-Africanism to expose the already strained health resources of one African country to unaffordable large numbers of foreign citizens. A desirable pan-African agenda should be rooted in the constructs of Ubuntu which would allow a state to share from surplus available resources as opposed to 'taking' from citizens.

A former Police Minister openly lamented the scourge of illegal migrant criminals in South Africa. The Police Minister hinted on the use of ex-military personnel from foreign countries in criminal acts that include cash-in-transit robberies and automated teller machine bombings within South Africa. The minister was expressing a frustration that the police were finding it difficult to trace and apprehend undocumented migrant criminals. The country has recently witnessed a police officer getting murdered by illegal migrants. More determined measures on irregular migration were expected from the state after this family man was killed by undesirable persons in South Africa. It is also notable that representatives of the Zimbabwean Community living in SA were reported to have issued a statement condemning the atrocious acts by some of their countrymen. The expat movement extended messages of condolence to the family of the deceased, the SAPS as well as South African citizens, noting that such criminal acts fuel negative perceptions towards all migrants (ANA, 2020). The position on adherence to the rule of law by expats in SA should be the minimum standard amongst diaspora formations to fight against the ills of irregular migration into South Africa. This matter importantly points to the grave danger that men and women in the armed forces face when the state turns a blind eye to irregular migration. South African communities have also raised concerns on the security risk posed by the number of irregular migrants seen to occupy any vacant land and mountains in the country. The reality today is that some of the illegal migrant land occupiers appear in local courts after being arrested for killing and maiming unsuspecting South Africans.

A serving labour Minister spoke strongly against the prioritisation of foreign nationals in non-scarce jobs that unemployed South Africans can occupy. He condemned this practice amidst the high unemployment rate in South Africa. The Minister also noted that employers who prefer foreign nationals do so to possibly flout existing labour laws in relation to wages and conditions of employment. He impressed upon his ministry and department to be tough in dealing with such practices as local jobseekers would never allow themselves to be overlooked in employment, where such dissatisfactions could disrupt peace among communities. The Minister further pointed out that poor migrants find themselves trapped in economic hardships which required hard talk among leaders of the region (DEL, 2019a). The true version of pan-Africanism is espoused in African leaders who are bold to speak out when things go wrong between Africans. The unity of Africa stands to benefit from the mutual respect for the rule of law in all countries within the continent (AU, 2018).

While he may not have had presidential powers, one former mayor of Johannesburg was very firm in prioritising South African needs and acting against illegal immigration. There were several attempts to silence this leader. The mayor lamented the scourge of illegal migration which exacerbated efforts to provide adequate housing and other services to citizens. He was also outspoken about the plight of undocumented migrants who fall prey to human trafficking and enslavement activities. He further referred to tensions which arise within communities due to increased competition from migrants (Joint Parliamentary Committees, 2019).

A prominent King in South Africa was also taken to the South African Human Rights Commission (SAHRC) for expressing an opinion on the growing numbers of immigrants in South Africa (SAHRC, 2016). The continued attempts to silence South Africa's leaders from speaking against reckless immigration, has the potential to irritate ordinary citizens. We must note that when leaders are prevented from speaking out, then citizens will speak and take action, with possible disastrous consequences. Expatriates who occupy positions of influence in South Africa are expected to also speak out in defence of the unity of Africa which should be pillared on the respect for sovereign laws of all African countries.

A young leader of a new political party in South Africa's parliament has advocated consistently and strongly for the township and rural economies to be reserved primarily for citizens. This focus is important as the official statistical body has also indicated that employment in the informal economy was already more favourable for immigrants at 29% compared to locals at 17% as far back as 2017 (StatsSA, 2019). Ordinary South Africans have also been calling some radio stations alluding to the risk that cheap labour poses to the availability of jobs, only to be told by some radio presenters that their observations were only anecdotal and not based on empirical evidence. The irony with this kind of discourse is that a broadcaster dismisses a complaint as not widespread without advancing empirical evidence to contradict the listener's experience as isolated.

Many South Africans are breaking their silence on the carnage caused by irregular migration on the country's job market and limited resources. The current coronavirus (covid-19) lockdown restrictions have prompted many to go onto social media platforms to protest the prioritisation of immigrants in South Africa's job market. Social media has provided identity safety net for people who might ordinarily not publicly voice their protests on unacceptable state conduct. A state that cares deeply about addressing any gross discomfort of citizens may not want to silence such freedoms of expression but utilise these outlets to assess existing narratives on contentious matters. Xenophobia has been used as a label to silence ordinary South Africans and their leaders from demanding prioritisation in their own country, something that all other countries on the continent and beyond do without being similarly stigmatised.

3.3 Summarising comments

The observed disparities in reactions towards the prioritisation of domestic needs by African states are negatively tilted against South Africa:

→ African states do prioritise their own citizens above all others without getting stigmatised as being anti-immigrant or xenophobic.

→ There is an observed desperation to silence South Africa's leaders and citizens from speaking out on the negative effects of uncontrolled immigration on sovereign limited resources.

→ The state's inaction on irregular migration in South Africa has fatal consequences for all families who lose their loved ones at the hands of illegal migrants.

4. The Fight for Limited Jobs in SA

4.1 Protests for jobs by the unemployed in SA

It is reasonable to mention that some of the violence between migrants and locals that erupted in South Africa relating to jobs might have been avoided if the state paid more attention to what the official statistical reports showed.

During 2019 some local truck driver organisations resorted to violence in expressing their dissatisfaction on the continued employment of foreign nationals as truck drivers to the exclusion of unemployed South Africans. This spate of violent protests that saw the burning of several trucks in this country was also acknowledged through statements by a joint ministerial task team made up of the Minister of Police, the Minister of Transport and the Minister of Employment and Labour (SAPS, 2019d). The protesters were correctly citing *Section 18(3)(a) of the Immigration Regulations 2014 and Section 8 of the Employment Services Act, which prohibit the employment of immigrants in non-scarce jobs that unemployed locals can occupy.* In this case still, the contents of the StatsSA (2019) report were possibly never brought up for discussion as it would confirm that the local truck drivers were correct to protest against many immigrants getting prioritised in local jobs. The trucking industry impasse reared its ugly head again in July 2020 with local truck drivers protesting against the same issues as in the previous year. Despite various laws which support the demands of the protests, the state still showed lack of will to simply enforce existing laws to protect the livelihoods of their citizens.

During 2019 more South Africans became radicalised and carried guns going around construction sites in protests demanding employment as many construction companies were seen to exclude local jobseekers. They further rejected the seeming proliferation of non-local business operators getting state tenders to do construction projects to the exclusion of local black business entities (Watermayer and Phillips, 2020). These formations were in essence lamenting the brazen violation of *regulation 9 of the Preferential Procurement Regulations* crafted in line with *Section 5 of the Preferential Procurement Policy Framework Act, Immigration and Labour laws that were meant to prioritise the interests of citizens.* Some media houses were quick to label these South Africans as the construction mafia. Sadly, one must wonder whether the Presidency would have informed any cabinet minister or even the construction industry stakeholders that they were in possession of an official statistical report that confirmed the 'deadly' employment trends that citizens were protesting against.

4.2 Community-wide protests for jobs in SA

When the State fails to provide leadership in the protection of the local job market, then ordinary citizens will fill that vacuum with protests. Generally, when protests break out, it becomes easy for some politicians and media to attach their own descriptions and condemnations to such events, often far removed from the real substance of the protest.

In 2017, Mamelodi residents in Gauteng protested strongly against retail shops that employed many foreign nationals in non-scarce jobs while there were many unemployed locals. In response to that protest, the Department of Home Affairs (DHA) issued statements that the retail shops alleged to have violated the country's Immigration and Labour laws were getting investigated. It was further announced by the DHA (2017) that illegal foreign nationals and store managers were arrested in that regard. There was no noticeable attempt by the state to deny or deflect the realities of what the protest demanded. It is therefore fair to say that state intervention in that protest was pointed and effective.

A State is like a parent charged with raising children to become decent and fulfilled members of society. On many instances, children tend to go back and do the same wrong things for which they were previously punished. South Africa is still a young democracy and this comes with huge responsibilities for individual and corporate citizens to work harder to stop breaking existing laws. When we mature without the rule of law, we would simply become a mature criminal state posing a wider risk to others within our ecosystem.

It is crucial that in our journey as a growing democracy, we spare some time to reflect on what can be learned from events such as the Mamelodi protest. The following observations may help:

a) The State listened to its citizens and immediately attended to the problem. There was clear feedback on what corrective course of action was taken. This is ideally how a government department should behave in addressing contentious issues raised by citizens.

b) The retail stores that were found to have flouted the law did not attempt to spin some justification for their illegal activities, at least not publicly. They simply complied with the punitive measures meted out to them. This is how a corporate citizen should behave, that when you mess up you fix it and start doing the right thing.

c) The State did not get unduly heavy-handed on the accused retail stores. They instead displayed a maturity that understood the huge economic role still to be played by those retailers. This is how a state that is committed to a growing economy should behave.

d) The illegal migrants who were found to be working at these stores also complied with the punitive measures imposed by the state. They did not run to some human rights or diaspora forum to try to blackmail a sovereign state to impose their illegal presence in the country. This is how a fellow human being behaves, that when you are caught committing unlawful acts in a foreign country you humble yourself and accept the consequences. This shows respect for South Africa and her citizens, it also shows respect for your country of origin and other expats, because negative generalisations about immigrants develop on account of a few lawless and arrogant individuals.

e) The protesting South Africans did not remain in the streets indefinitely even after their government undertook to address their complaints. That protest could have claimed a lot of casualties because of the sensitivities associated with immigration. We should be proud of those who protest and still respect the sanctity of human life, an attribute commonly mistaken for weakness when it is in essence the hallmark of greatness in a nation.

Through this protest, Mamelodi residents played a huge oversight role in our politics and economy. Our democracy would therefore be best served if communities of South Africa would maintain the same kind of vigilance and activism.

4.3 Summarising comments

The perceived lacklustre intervention by the state to stop the carnage caused by irregular migration in South Africa has already breached tolerance levels among citizens:

➜ Unemployed local truck drivers are already protesting the prioritisation of foreign visa holders in violation of local laws.

➜ Unemployed locals are already protesting the prioritisation of immigrants and non-local contractors in the construction industry.

➜ Communities have already started protesting the employment of immigrants in retail jobs that unemployed citizens can occupy.

5. The Risk of Ignoring official Statistics and Laws

5.1 The role of official statistics

When official statistics get ignored, then all sentiment about establishing early warning systems on potential unrest areas in the country ring hollow. StatsSA is already South Africa's reliable early warning facility and leaders who ignore this entity's empirical reports will undoubtedly expose this country to enormous risk. A state that is serious about meeting the needs of citizens would constantly ensure that their official statistical agency is well funded and resourced. Political leaders who are not informed on populations they have solemnly sworn to serve should simply be seen as dishonest in their commitment to put communities above self. Let us remember that official statistics exist to give leaders a glimpse of what might happen in the future based on past experience. Choosing to ignore such official indicators would not eliminate the possible outcome, it would only render the decision maker to be un-prepared to deal with predicted eventualities. Many people are lately expressing discomfort on South Africa's worsening immigration crisis, when StatsSA had already sounded this warning early through their official reports.

There have been disturbing trends where representatives of expats in SA would simply dismiss the worries of locals around jobs and services as xenophobia and not based on empirical evidence. Many so-called analysts masquerading as scholars with doctorates, have tried to suppress local sentiments against the devastation caused by irregular migration. We now realise they could just be charlatans, as the reports and laws that are cited in this book have been available from government since their release. It could also be that people think South Africans are fools, taking the cue from political leaders, who have access to such empirical reports but are not keen to enforce existing laws. This attitude was never to be sustainable because access to information has improved for many ordinary citizens. People could soon rise in a rebellion if the ruling party does not rein in their deployed officials to uphold the laws of this country to protect citizens and resources.

Currently nobody seems to have a clue how many illegal migrants are in South Africa. This should alarm all residents in this country including the properly documented foreign guests. It is highly recommended for state leaders to factor-in the prevailing official statistical trends in all their decisions to allow for equitable allocation of limited resources.

5.2 Emergence of a parallel state

A parallel state is described as a clandestine link between formal political leadership, self-serving factions within the state apparatus and organised crime. Such a parallel arrangement is usually meant to distort the implementation of official government policy by protecting and promoting the interests of factions that enjoy deep and lasting links to the state as well as to outsiders who specialise in violence (Briscoe, 2008). Clientelism on the other hand is a relationship based on political subordination in exchange for material rewards. This phenomenon is best explained in a situation where political candidates running for office use various incentives including money to sway voter choices to favour the vote-buyer. It amounts to subversion of democracy since voters would in essence be coerced through money to choose less preferred candidates to occupy influential positions and possibly pursue less favoured agendas (Fox, 2012).

One of the effects of a parallel state is the inability of official government to provide needed services due to resources getting diverted towards minority interests. South Africans must probe how their state intends to run public affairs when official statistics and a string of laws get ignored and violated to the point where protests by citizens are normalised. Even in the heat of such protests, the Constitution which compels the state to implement existing legislative instruments also gets ignored. So, all have to wonder whether the official South Africa Inc is beholden to dubious faceless others.

The following possible enabling activities in a parallel state should be **stopped if they exist**, as such would explain why some (political leaders and employers) seem heavily incentivised to break existing local and international laws:

a) Politicians who encourage and exploit irregular migration to obtain illegal votes from migrants using fraudulent citizenship documents. This could happen where politicians fail to deliver election promises to the local electorate, thus attempt to create fresh constituencies from immigrants. Such treasonous conduct would grossly violate *Section 19(2) and (3) of the Constitution of SA which affirms the right of citizens to free and fair regular elections to vote for their sovereign leaders.* Citizens of other countries who get used for political regime change in this manner would be further violating *Article 4(g) of the Constitutive Act of the AU which entrenches non-interference by any member state in the internal affairs of another. Article 4(p) condemns and rejects unconstitutional changes of governments.* To ensure that a sovereign voters roll is not corrupted, members of the armed forces together with community representatives may have to be involved with the IEC[11] to closely monitor elections to root out carriers of fraudulent identity documents on the day of elections.

b) Politicians or individuals who engage in cheap labour brokering

---

[11] IEC is the Independent Electoral Commission

activities masked as registered employment agencies. The slave conditions of cheap labourers are a violation of *Section 13 of the Constitution which prohibits slavery and servitude*. The practice of trafficking migrants into the local economy and *collecting unlawful fees from their wages is a violation of Section 15(1) and (4) of the Employment Services Act which prohibits such fees*. The principles and guidelines of the ILO (2020a) also discourage such wage deductions. These activities push local jobseekers out of employment thus plunging local families into abject poverty and further promote human trafficking[12] crimes.

c) Business entities that rely on the 'cheap labour' supplied through the broker referred to in paragraph (b) to unlawfully cut labour costs. Such arrangements would have been concluded by violating *Section 23 of the Constitution which guarantees worker access to fair labour practices and Section 13 which prohibits slavery*.

d) Politicians who subvert existing sovereign laws by keeping silent on irregular migration or develop instant regulations to legalise unlawful practices in exchange for personal business deals in foreign countries.

e) Private persons who benefit from bribes paid for illegal entry into South Africa. Such persons would fraudulently issue

---

[12] DEL (2020b). *Media statement: JHB magistrates court to hear the application for leave to appeal the bail in the Chinese human trafficking and violation of SA labour laws case.* Pretoria: DEL

official visas for cash. Some would identify unofficial openings along the border fence and demand cash for unlawful entry and exit between countries. This conduct contributes to cross-border theft and other criminality. When countries officially restrict international movements during the covid-19 pandemic, this phenomenon undermines such efforts thus exposing sovereign states to deadly infections.

The undeterred machinations of a parallel state could contribute to normalising illegal activities which are ordinarily prohibited by well-known existing laws. When state leaders turn a blind eye to widespread illegality, it could be due to their involvement in organizing, approving and benefiting from such criminality!

5.3 Summarising comments

Official statistics are characterised by internationally endorsed methodologies which give credence to their reliability and integrity.

→ Politicians must pay attention to official statistics to base their decisions on empirically sound information.
→ Violation and non-enforcement of existing laws by the state contributes to the increase in lawlessness by citizens and guests.

6. Escalating Tensions due to Inaction

6.1 Migration and resources

If a state does not take interest in addressing complaints on irregular migration, then ordinary citizens would eventually do something chaotic about it. The many service delivery protests may be an indication beyond statistics that South Africa has been overwhelmed by irregular migration. This situation could create room for undesirable interventions by ordinary citizens.

The resources that get plundered when a state turns a blind eye to irregular migration, are much more than job losses:

a) The constitutionally mandated safety and security of all citizens and documented immigrants get compromised as unknown numbers of illegal migrant criminals could start choosing South Africa as their preferred playground. Communities would be under siege as police reports and media show how irregular migrants add to the high crime statistics of rape, murder, robberies, hijacking, drug trafficking, cable theft, railway line theft and illegal electricity connections. This would be a violation of *Section 12 of the Constitution which affirms the right to security for all persons and freedom from violence from any sources.*

b) The provision in *Section 26 of the Constitution for access to adequate housing* is possibly violated and could become an unachievable target as unknown numbers of migrants join locals to set up shacks to settle on any vacant land and occupy empty buildings in South Africa. Irregular migration would add to the burden of housing provision, leading to people sharing accommodation in large numbers, creating squalor conditions in violation of disease control protocols and bylaws. This conduct could create a platform for violence around land risking the ignition of a civil war which was avoided in 1994.

c) Health care provision could grind to a stand-still as unknown numbers of irregular migrants join locals to access clinics and hospitals that were already not sufficiently equipped to cater for South African citizens. The unabated overload of health care access perpetuates the violation of *Section 27 of the Constitution which guarantees citizens' right to access health care services.*

d) The country's education system could collapse as lawful learning centres get overcrowded leading to the possible proliferation of illegal schools in South Africa. The education funding meant for South African citizens would get unfairly stretched to include irregular migrants thus putting a further strain on the limited coffers of SA. *Section 29 of the Constitution proclaims the right of citizens to basic and further education.*

e) South Africa's social security system designed to help the poorest citizens through various monetary grants, could face enormous pressure as many poor migrants push to also access the same limited social grants. The collapse of Social Services would lead to a violation of *Section 27 of the Constitution affirming citizens' right to social security.*

f) *Section 27(2) of the Constitution compels the state to take reasonable legislative and other measures, within available resources to achieve the progressive realisation of the rights of citizens to healthcare, food, water and social security.* If the state fails to enforce existing legislation meant to regularise migration, thereby leading to large numbers of irregular migrants adding pressure on available sovereign resources, then the state could have violated *Section 27(2) of the Constitution.*

g) The inaction of a sovereign state in taking preventative measures to discourage irregular migration may contribute as a pull factor in attracting more poor desperate human beings into a slave market. This would lead to a violation of *Article 4 of the UDHR which prohibits all forms of slavery and slave trade. Section 13 of the Constitution of SA also prohibits slavery, servitude or forced labour.*

h) Importantly, the unity of Africa will be derailed when citizens of one country illegally enter another sovereign state in violation of sovereign laws. *Article 3(a) of the Constitutive Act of the AU declares the commitment to achieve greater unity and solidarity between African countries and the peoples of Africa. Article 3(b) declares the commitment of AU to protect the sovereignty, territorial integrity and independence of its member states.*

6.2 Undesirable possibilities

It was only fair for a regulated number of people from other countries to arrive in South Africa to celebrate and enjoy the trappings of her democracy, given that we were all fighting a common enemy during colonialism. South Africans have always welcomed people from across the continent and the world to enjoy the rich and diverse local cultures while carving livelihoods. This meeting of kindred souls on SA soil was unfortunately poisoned by the continued violation of immigration protocols meant to illicit the best experience for both visitors and hosts. The state should take responsibility for the missed opportunity in managing this re-union of homo-sapiens in SA. One may argue that SA could comfortably share some jobs and some resources without fracturing, had the state paid attention to the numbers involved. There can be 'no state without stats.'

6.2.1 Class action lawsuit

An avenue for citizens who constantly suffer social and economic abuses by the state could be to institute a class action lawsuit against their president. Official statistical reports that a president receives to guide him on policy shifts could be used as hard empirical evidence in such a lawsuit. A sitting president may become liable for things going wrong while he may have had sufficient early warning to avert disaster. The injuries and death related to squabbles on jobs and resources between locals and migrants could be blamed on a president's failure to effectively address problems beforehand. The constitution and all laws that get violated could be used to build such a case. Such a lawsuit could have the same effect as a referendum to test the public's confidence in a sitting president.

If this option gets initialised, it could indicate the end to an era of self-serving individuals desperately running to occupy high office. The ruling party could defend their president at the risk of being ditched by the electorate with the possible accompanying rolling mass protests. The most efficient response would be to recall their deployed official as the manoeuvre would likely restore voter confidence and bring peace and stability in the country and the region.

6.2.2   Law enforcement by citizens

Another undesirable possibility would be for citizens to enforce their own laws. We should accept that when citizens get neglected by their state, there is a great deal of dehumanisation that besets such communities. In other words, when elected and appointed officials fail to solve societal problems, then people tend to suspend the known tenets of humanity and resort to deal with issues through any means necessary. Communities could start issuing notices to illegal migrants to leave the country voluntarily in for violating immigration and other laws in SA. Millions of unemployed citizens could join protests for the immediate prioritisation of South Africans in their own job market. This could include physically preventing any foreign employee from doing general work that unemployed locals can do. Businesses and employers who prefer cheap migrant labour over locals could also be targeted by angry jobless citizens to close for betraying local families while trading on South African soil.

It is known that when communities get angry at perceived illegal activities, they tend to swiftly mete out their own justice where people get hurt. While this fact might work as a compliance boost in the minds of perceived perpetrators, it would also be utterly inhumane to instil fear in the hearts and minds of many poor migrants whose home countries are thousands of kilometres away from SA. A further downside of this consideration is the humanitarian crisis that would follow because of millions of immigrants having to exit a country within a short space of time as in cases of war. The targeted businesses would also suffer huge disruptions and losses of income.

The deep moral question is whether angry citizens would at that point care about the humanitarian or business concerns of those perceived to have repeatedly and unlawfully engaged in activities aimed at ripping off South African livelihoods. Apart from a few exiled members of the liberation movements, the majority of South Africans remained in their apartheid riddled country and continued with protests against the apartheid criminal regime. Even though they were poor and abused, South Africans did not flood any job market in any part of the world with cheap labour. Those who became independent before SA were therefore given the space to enjoy and, in some cases, destroy their own countries as they saw fit. The notion that South Africa has to suspend the rule of law and order because a handful of exiled locals were hosted in controlled spaces in other countries is repulsive.

Any country in the world can be taken over without gunfire, through irregular migration. If the commander-in-chief of all armed forces sits quietly projecting a 'stand down' demeanour, protected by the same powerful military resource meant to safeguard the sovereignty of the state, then citizens would be justified to hold him accountable for his inaction. The armed forces in South Africa, made up of both the police and the army could also begin to refuse obeying any orders meant to stop citizens from enforcing state laws which politicians constantly violate. We often forget that the men and women of the armed forces are citizens and they too witness the devastation caused by irregular migration into their country. They have families and children who deserve a secure South Africa where the coming generations of descendants would stand to inherit a safe country. *Section 24 of the Constitution guarantees the rights of citizens to live in a protected environment through legislation for the benefit of present and future generations.*

The army and the police possess ground intelligence, the means and the proximity to arrest politicians who deliberately squander the sovereignty of SA for selfish gains, thereby enabling conflicts between poor locals and migrants. They too as guardians of a constitutional democracy could receive wide support in using all means necessary to protect their country from rogue politicians. It is in any case morally and tactically most efficient to apprehend a handful of irresponsible politicians than to control a justified country-wide rebellion.

6.2.3 Large scale rebellion

The scariest possibility to face South Africa and the entire continent would be a rebellion by poor citizens against the abuse perpetrated by the ruling elite. It is a fact that South Africans and foreign nationals have lived reasonably peacefully side by side for a number of years.

Significant relationships have developed among ordinary citizens of the continent as poor locals and foreigners shared common horror stories of their respective repressive governments. This friendship of the poor forged on South African soil gives rise to the probability of a mass mobilisation against state abuse on the continent.

The Arab-Spring[13] was a series of mass protests that took place in the Middle East and North Africa from 2010. Several countries were affected by these mass demonstrations as citizens lamented gross economic and social hardships imposed by their governments. Some of the presidents of the affected countries had to step down because military forces started to refuse the impossible task of clamping down on the continuous large-scale protests. There were also countries that took quick action to quell minor protests by conceding to some of the demands of citizens which included the dismissal of unwanted office bearers and constitutional reforms.

The SADC[14] countries could face a rebellion so massive and ferocious to make the Arab-Spring look like a picnic. Governments could be toppled, and corrupt politicians driven out to exile. Economies could be totally destroyed, and the decadence of political elitism vanquished. Indeed, all the above would equate to self-destruction, a suicide theme which is not entirely far-fetched in the minds of poor people who have nothing to lose. Terrorist activities and formations are also conceived in the womb of destitution.

---

[13] Encyclopaedia Britannica Editors (2019). *Arab Spring: pro-democracy protests.* Encyclopaedia Britannica Inc.

[14] SADC represents the Southern African Development Community comprised of several countries.

6.3 Summarising comments

→ Irregular migration contributes to tensions and instability within a host country.

→ Inaction in curbing irregular migration contributes to bitterness towards the state and migrants.

→ Lack of will to address lawful demands by citizens could eventually lead to extreme violence in protests or a nation-wide rebellion against the state.

7. State Intervention

7.1 Implementing existing laws

It is an observed phenomenon that many countries in Africa where the state shows firm leadership on immigration matters do not experience significant violence between migrants and local citizens. As briefly shown before, African governments have directly intervened through state presidents and ministers to assert their own immigration laws to protect their resources and citizens, thereby effectively reducing immigration confrontations among civilians. This approach has also saved ordinary African lives seen to be lost in South Africa's immigration squabbles. The lawful basis for the state to reverse the scourge of irregular migration in SA is as follows:

a) To inform all illegal migrants to leave the country on their own accord for violating immigration and other sovereign laws. The voluntary departure of illegal migrants would also preserve huge state resources spent on deportations. The stately approach would ensure that proper planning is in place for the orderly and safe departure of many illegal migrants as ratified in *Goal 10.7 within the United Nations SDGs.*

b) To reduce the issue and renewal of general work visas in line with *Section 18 of the Immigration Regulations 2014.* This practice could be one of the causes of violence between unemployed locals and migrant visa holders. This embargo could be temporary until the state is satisfied that the local unemployment rate is significantly lowered in favour of citizens. *Goal 10.7 of the United Nations SDGs urges governments to enhance safe migration through enforcing well planned migration policies,* such as existing legislation.

c) To inform those who have expired visas to also leave the country in line with *Section 43 of the Immigration Act as amended by Section 22 of Act 13 of 2011 that places the responsibility on migrants to ensure that they comply with all conditions of their stay and depart upon expiry of their visas.*

d) To educate all organs of state to comply with *Section 44 of the Immigration Act as amended by Section 42 of Act 19 of 2004 in ascertaining the citizenship when possible, of all who access such facilities for services and inform the Director General of Home Affairs about illegal migrants without infringing their rights.* This would also ensure that the burden of enforcement is not left to a single under-staffed department.

e) To warn the business sector to prioritise the employment of South Africans in accordance with *Section 18 of the Immigration Regulations 2014* and stop fronting migrants in their transformation positions. To side-line locals in their own country fuels hatred towards expats in SA. The business sector is crucial in availing jobs to unemployed locals to avoid a rebellion that could easily turn into a fight for land, thus reversing all the peace that SA has enjoyed in the past 26 years.

By providing focussed leadership on immigration, the state can ensure that the dignity of all affected migrants is protected. To do nothing when immigration issues get out of hand, would be disregard for the spirit and intent of the *Immigration Act expressed in paragraph (b) of the Preamble to ensure that state security is maintained.* South African leaders brokered an unbelievable peace deal when many expected bloodshed and mayhem at the birth of democracy. It is therefore not a mere pipe dream to expect humane presidential immigration solutions from the current leadership.

7.2 A considerate Afrocentric approach

All propositions hinted so far would never override the fact that we are dealing with fellow human beings whose struggles may not have been fully comprehended and appreciated. As Africans we must start considering the responsibility for doing everything within our capability to dedicate resources for the rehabilitation of wayward Africans as opposed to the usual punitive and expensive measures such as incarceration, expulsion or deportation. It is also reality that Africans face rejection in various parts of the world due to racism and bad conduct by Africans. Even the bad Africans originate from this continent, so they belong here. There is therefore a need to rekindle Africa's moral integrity to actively pave the way for the envisaged unity within the continent. This is important because if Africans do not re-generate and commit to their collective morality and responsibilities, there would still be constant strife and divisions within the continent for many years beyond colonialism. In line with this posture, the state could as an interim measure, only institute an immediate embargo on the issuing or renewal of all work visas until South Africa's labour market shows significant improvement in favour of local citizens. DEL (2019a) already supported 'regional measures' which could be urgently explored to deal comprehensively and decisively with illegal migration and criminality. It is a known African cultural practice for elders to be held accountable for the misbehaviour of their offspring. This should form the basis for demanding accountability and corrective action from foreign government leaders and diplomats for the misconduct of their citizens in host countries. It would not be too far-fetched as it is widely accepted that people sometimes adopt irregular/illegal means just to get away from abusive states. Other suggested interventions could also be considered as discussed in Section 9.2 of this book.

7.3 Summarising comments

→ The state should take urgent measures to eliminate irregular migration as it poses a risk to state security and limited resources.

→ As opposed to the usual promise of developing more robust legislation to deal with current problems, the state should ease prevailing tensions by simply enforcing current laws.

8. The continent of Africa

8.1 Africa's unity

The acceptance of western governance methods and structures on the African continent has unfortunately led to Africa rejecting her indigenous ways. The self-sacrifices and concessions have been many and consistent for centuries resulting in Africans being seen as lesser citizens at the world trade table. It is most likely that Africa's disunity and self-doubt played a significant role in the social and economic degradation of the continent. To exorcise the post-colonial demons of self-hate, Africans need to spend time and resources to resuscitate indigenous knowledge systems upon which to draw for the road to complete emancipation (Zaamout, 2020). Many African countries have within the post-independence dispensation, shamelessly continued with the demotion of traditional leadership structures and ways, into total subordination to western systems. Indigenous Africans still take pride in being excellent speakers of western languages than their own, consequently elevating such non-African languages as preferred tools in social and economic discourse (Abraham, 2020). It is also worrying that Africans still see their economic worth as prescribed through western capitalistic views which seem to exclude the intuitively known tenets of Ubuntu, which include respect and compassion. The concept and practice of Ubuntu could be an opportune rally point to unite Africans in ways that promote communal gains thereby forging a human centred pan-Africanism. This is important because the exposure of Africans in the diaspora and in the continent to the joys of capitalism could have diluted the intended spirit of a pan-African movement that should be pro-poor. The seeming inability of Africa to adopt economic ideologies that exalt humanity above profit could be further indication that African elites may be defending capitalism for their own class preservation (Fagunwa, 2019). To unleash the potential embedded in Ubuntu there is a need to expand this concept beyond Africa as an ideology for global moral re-generation. To tout Africa as the cradle of humankind without accepting her indigenous cultures as worthy of world-wide emulation, would amount to a twisted logic. It is therefore rational to motivate world communities to embrace for example, the practice of honouring ancestral activity as a tool to guide future generations in appealing to facets of Ubuntu for preserving the co-existence of humans and their habitat (Van Breda, 2019).

African slaves were preferred in the world market because of their sheer strength and resilience. As defined by the American Psychological Association (2014), resilience is the process of adapting well in the face of adversity, trauma, tragedy, threats, or even significant sources of stress. It is possible to exploit people's readiness to adapt to difficulties, coupled with Ubuntu which somewhat guarantees non-violent resistance to abuse over extended time periods. For Africa to thrive without abandoning her human attributes there is a need to draw a thick line to stop all economic parasites from taking advantage of the warm-hearted indigenous cultures, to again rob this continent of her resources and glory.

In 1884, several leaders from western countries gathered in Berlin to discuss ways in which they could share parts of the continent of Africa. This meeting among colonisers, also known as the Berlin Conference, excluded all African representation (Craven, 2015). What is important for Africans to take from this conference is that western colonisers chose to stop fighting each other to unite for the takeover of Africa for material exploitation. That Berlin objective was achieved and so Africans must focus on their unity as that could be the only way to liberate the continent from the economic clutches of the colonial hangover. While the Berlin gang left the continent with imposed borders, it is also true that Africa had its own demarcation processes which for many years ensured that different empires, monarchies and tribes co-existed by sharing mutual respect for each other's rules and cultures. This collective acceptance of equitable access to common ecosystems was not negotiable as violations of any self-determined spaces, would lead to wars between different African groupings.

Importantly, *Articles 3(b) and 4(b) of the Constitutive Act of the African Union* (AU) *declares the commitment of this continental body to respect the borders existing on achievement of independence and defend the sovereignty, territorial integrity and independence of its member states* (AU, 2000). This means that all African countries have chosen to recognise and work with existing colonial borders. Citizens of Africa therefore have a joint responsibility to ensure the realisation of these legislative provisions. While a borderless Africa is not a bad idea, what would not be acceptable is to propagate for collapsing the borders and related laws of one country while others remain as sovereign states.

8.2 Respect for South Africa's sovereignty

South Africa like any other geographic space on the planet is a land of opportunity. The key is to avoid trashing those opportunity prospects. The debate about 'a borderless Africa' is a good example to consider in this discussion. The topic itself is important and relevant yet the timing and place should also be appropriate. When an illegal migrant gets arrested for being in a country without proper documentation, it would not be the right time to advocate for a borderless Africa. When one is already in another country illegally, it would not be the right place to share ideas on a united Africa. It is better to show respect towards existing laws than try to persuade a sovereign state to change laws that you already violate. No sovereign country will entertain pressure from un-invited persons trying to change existing laws to suit non-citizens. Political leaders risk being violently removed from office through country-wide protests against subverting existing laws to please visitors at the expense of citizens. *Article 3, Sections (1) and (2) of the AU Protocol on free movement in the continent, declares that cross border movements should be based on the respect for laws and policies, and on the protection of national security, public order, public health, the environment and any other factors that would be detrimental to the host state* (AU, 2018).

The unity of Africa will not be best served by expatriates who speak boldly and loudly about a borderless Africa when they are in South Africa and never in their countries of origin. The fact that the topic on a borderless Africa never comes up as strongly in other African countries who achieved their independence way before South Africa seems opportunistic. It would be in the continent's best interest for the AU to put this topic on their agenda to initiate a structured debate by member states. This will help to provide continental leadership and clarity thus undermine opportunistic pronouncements by wannabe gurus of pan-Africanism.

South Africa remains to be the go-to-place by many for economic survival and better livelihoods. If Africans work together to respect and preserve this country, we might stand a good chance to rehabilitate other broken countries on the continent. Coming into SA forcefully and lawlessly will irritate locals into a retaliation which would further delay continental unity efforts. It is critical to be sufficiently vigilant to separate genuine calls for unity from politically expedient rhetoric. Even the most ambitious of political advocates for a united borderless Africa, do submit themselves to abiding by all immigration and sovereign laws of any country that they visit. All who genuinely care about Africa should work towards a continental unity which is pillared upon the rule of law, orderly conduct and respect for others.

8.3 Is South Africa ready for expats to occupy high office?

It seems easy for people from other countries to occupy positions in South Africa's parliament, which is one of the highest portfolios in the land while SA citizens have not held any political leadership position in any independent state in the world. It is highly probable that South Africa is still reasonably intact as a country compared to others because her citizens wisely agreed to a peaceful settlement into independence instead of confrontation. It should be laudable for a nation to continue adopting political, social and economic solutions that protect the sanctity of human life above all else (AU, 2000). In line with the *Traditional Leadership and Governance Framework Act*, local traditional leaders (Queens, Kings and Chiefs) have agreed to submit to the authority of the democratic state and by extension this meant taking directives from men and women who serve in Parliament, the Executive and the Judiciary (South Africa, 2003). To expect the country's royal fraternity and citizens to suddenly be lead through parliament by youngsters who originate from other countries could be a little too much too soon!

The high-horse posture taken by some of the world leaders, who have openly ridiculed SA's reconciliation approach to independence and be-little the country as some kind of a junior state is problematic. Such negative sentiments could have influenced ordinary citizens and followers of the leaders referred to. This would then present a possible risk in including unbelievers of 'multiracial democracies' in strategic positions to lead and nurture SA's reconciliation project. This matter deserves a presidential debate. In the meantime, expat leaders serving in parliament and influential positions could be subjected to training aimed at fostering a culture of tolerance and acceptance of South Africa's inclusive democracy. The right of a child born in one country to aspire to be president of another country is a light and fluffy sign of confidence that should be encouraged by all adults in that child's space. Adults should however have an urgent debate on the readiness of current geo-political ecosystems to accommodate such borderless dreams, because there are children in all countries who dream of being presidents in their own countries. The potential for hatred due to the infringement of 'personal space' should not be ignored. Such matters deserve to be properly ventilated as there could be sweet explanations yearning to be heard. Who knows, children's dreams could be just the trigger that the world needs to shift existing paradigms towards acceptable modes of globalism. We must work towards eliminating possible hostilities towards expat leaders as there is already a pool of more than 55 million citizens in SA some of whom with aspirations to occupy high office in their own country. The African Union should entertain such continental discussions. It is undeniable that the peoples of the world are in love with the beautiful South Africa. Much as this heated affection for Mzansi is flattering, it does come with tight responsibilities; respect for her rules, ability to contribute meaningfully to her well-being and readiness to protect her from all harm. Just as it applies to all heavenly creatures of beauty, those who fall short of this minimum requirement will be kicked out, as they should!

8.4 Humility versus arrogance

Humble people generally get accepted in many circles, as they make everyone around them feel respected. The same cannot be said about the arrogance of man which provokes vile emotions and reactions in others. The conversation about 'who is more educated' is just a desperate egotistical trip among those haunted by untold insecurities. Their usual trick is to miniaturise everything around them just so they can feel like undisputed giants'. The intended continental unity would likely benefit from individual moral virtues such as open mindedness, compromise and cooperativeness in the pursuit of collective goals (Tanesini, 2020). The deception of elevating others as intelligent beings while robbing them blind is no longer a viable con. Such hollow praise can also be used for the destruction of entire economies and the exploitation of human desperation to enslave nations. A similar worrying modus operandi is possibly at play in South Africa, where jobs get offered to immigrants by telling them that they are smarter than locals, while they get stuck in 'slave conditions' with little prospects for career or personal growth. African people, who still subject themselves to be enslaved in any manner, are not contributing meaningfully to the overall emancipation of the continent from the effects of colonialism. We should all join hands to reclaim our place on the world stage as proud Africans who respect themselves enough to deserve the best that life has to offer, especially on African soil.

There is a simple yardstick to test educational progress. When education standards are indeed superior elsewhere, then the highly educated are not expected to destroy their own economies and livelihoods. Any useful education must transform the recipient into a more successful and self-respecting human being. Ironically, more immigrants who came into South Africa from 2012 do not have matric or equivalent educational standing (StatsSA, 2019). Ordinary Africans should individually commit themselves to respect each other before unity at continent level can be achieved. The small circle of the ruling elite across the continent are already united in their access and abuse of state resources.

8.5 Lazy South Africans

An insult casually hurled at locals to appease and justify the use of slave labourers, is that South Africans are lazy. It seems to be a minority of employed people and employers who resort to this kind of degradation towards jobless citizens.

There are currently millions of migrants living in South Africa for a variety of reasons. We have people fleeing from war-torn countries seeking asylum in SA. There are also economic migrants looking for better livelihoods in South Africa. We are also host to a handful of expats in possession of specialised skills that are needed to expand the economic horizon of any country. All these people came to South Africa and found a relatively good place with infrastructure much better than many other developing countries. All guests from other countries found relative peace among South Africans who chose to live together after a dark past of apartheid. The current beautiful South Africa came to exist through the blood and sweat of local citizens. Through the many years of colonial rule to date, local South Africans are fully credited for working this land to where it is today one of the most developed regions in Africa. Let us therefore be careful how we label those who forgive and welcome many to share their limited food. It should not be shocking to see continuous outcry by locals for better services when South Africa is already relatively better compared to other developing economies. Civilian oversight through activism is a democratic tool which must be consistently deployed to undermine the scourge of corruption by leaders. The loss of jobs and other services due to irregular migration is a real pain to locals and a threat to South Africa's democracy. All are therefore urged to refrain from insults, disrespect and racial slurs.

8.6 Zimbabwe's isolation

Zimbabwe was once respected as the breadbasket of the Southern regions of the continent of Africa. In the early years of Zimbabwe's independence, the world became aware of the Lancaster House Agreement which included Britain's commitment to help finance the land reform programmes in Zimbabwe. When Zimbabwean leaders reported to the entire world that Britain had not honoured their promise to provide some of the funding for land reform, not many paid attention. Some African countries offered some support to Zimbabwe's ruling party in that outcry. South Africa's leaders maintained that Zimbabwe was a sovereign country to be allowed to deal with her problems without interference. It is undeniable that some western leaders had intended to use South Africa's proximity to Zimbabwe as a conduit for regime change (Mbeki, 2016). Forceful land invasions in Zimbabwe triggered the imposition of economic sanctions by some western countries leading to that country being tagged as a failing state. The world would subsequently witness the Zimbabwean leadership at international gatherings, angrily telling western leaders to leave Zimbabwe alone. African leaders were also seen to applaud that level of rage, as it may have represented their silent disdain for the west. The same Africans must have also known that Zimbabwean delegates would receive hostile audiences from potential foreign investors at gala dinners during such international events. It cannot be brotherly love to cheer when one of your own rages in solo-protests against giant western economies without the commitment from the African collective to raise funds to put food on the Zimbabwean table. The isolation of Zimbabwe by African leaders would only ensure that the continent remained divided and open to economic vultures. Today, Zimbabweans are scattered all over the SADC region getting enslaved by the same African brotherhood.

8.7 Move to self-reliance

To redeem ourselves, the African Union must create a pool of funds to aggressively invest in broken economies on the continent. Setting up slave labour broker agencies that traffic poor migrants is not pan-Africanism, but sheer criminality driven by self-centred gains. Securing individualistic business deals across the continent by politicians is not pan-Africanism but greed. African leaders must commit to stopping the rampant looting of resources aimed at funding continental developments. South Africans are invited to realise that their deep dissatisfaction on jobs and resources is towards government leaders and not immigrants many of whom being visibly poor and downtrodden. We owe it to our humanity as ordinary citizens to help them where possible.

Africans have suffered indignity and rejection in many parts of the world, so we need a collective undertaking to respect sovereign laws of all countries that we visit to remain above reproach. The culture of violating sovereign laws by immigrants would still lead to tensions among Africans on the continent and further hamper efforts towards unity. South Africa will rise again, Zimbabwe will rise again, and Africa will unite. The President is charged with leading this nation and the continent to prosperity and peace pillared on the rule of law and respect for others. So, we pray.

8.8 Summarising comments

→ The unity of Africa should be based on mutual respect for the sovereignty of member states.

→ South Africa is a sovereign state with laws that should be respected by all within her borders.

→ Contrary to popular belief, citizens of South Africa are humble, intelligent and hospitable enough to steer clear of self-praise and hollow pride, which precede self-destruction.

→ Africans should help each through tough times.

9. Rebuilding 'a future we deserve'

9.1 The ruling party

The reality that South Africa still exists as a country with reasonable prospects for economic recovery bears positive testimony about the capabilities of the ruling party. For a political party that came into power in the early nineties with no prior experience in running a state, it would only be fair to credit the ruling party for significant sovereign achievements that were realised since 1994. All the laws and institutions which pertain to the democratic state were developed through the leadership of the ruling party.

In relation to the Decent Work Agenda discussed in section 2.6 earlier, the ruling party has successfully presided over the modest achievement of labour rights for more than 50% of the local workforce in each of the indicators on decent work (StatsSA, 2019). This hard evidence effectively means that several corporate citizens in SA do adhere to existing labour laws by availing good jobs devoid of abuses.

The ruling party had already expressed within the National Development Plan 2030 (NDP) a desire for relatively easing the movement of people between countries in Africa to spur regional and continental economic growth. The NDP sought to invoke a systematic approach to regional development as opposed to collapsing South Africa's borders through irregular migration. This position displays the kind of good leadership that one would expect from a ruling party, in stark contrast to the haphazard call for a borderless Africa. The NDP was also explicit on prioritising domestic needs within South Africa's foreign policy objectives. This stance was further amplified within this plan by specifically asserting the sharing of regional resources to avoid burdening any single country with unaffordable continental demands (National Planning Commission, 2012).

So, the need for existing migration control measures to be enforced to prioritise citizens and protect limited resources, is not a fresh concept within the ruling party. The problem seems to be with a minority of deployed officials who refuse to implement party directives. South Africans are therefore entitled to expect their ruling party to effectively deal with that minority to ensure that ratified agreements get urgently implemented to pull the country back onto a path to economic and social stability.

9.2 Exploring state sovereignty as an asset

Leaders and society should entertain discussions on how state sovereignty can be utilised as an asset. Such a debate could yield outcomes which ensure that every little piece of a country's sovereignty is disbursed as a prudent investment activity that stands to benefit ordinary citizens. This posture might help to allay fears around sovereignty being squandered by political leaders in return for individualistic gains. It would be important to first accept that the sovereignty asset would not belong to any single politician or even a president. The real shareholders of such an asset would collectively be citizens. All arms of the state in the form of the executive, parliament or the judiciary, would have to shoulder the responsibility of ensuring that state sovereignty is utilised to benefit all citizens.

For example, if a cabinet minister issues a lawful circular saying that thousands of migrants should be given visas to come into a sovereign state to trade for survival, then that minister should provide details of benefits that would accrue to ordinary citizens through this exercise. Mitigation against all possible adverse effects of such a decision would also have to be fully communicated. Bi-lateral migration deals could be openly negotiated to include ordinary citizens of countries involved so that the risks and benefits are understood and dealt with by broad society. The transparent approach could ease tensions and limit uninformed stereotypes between locals and migrants

A migration agreement could further allow for the same amount of land occupied by immigrants to be made available to host-country citizens wishing to explore opportunities in another country. This move could help to eliminate an uncontrolled spate of illegal land invasions by immigrants in a sovereign state. As already hinted within the NDP, a migration agreement could generally establish that all costs incurred by the host-country on immigrants be defrayed by the sending-country in cash or assets of equivalent value.

The above outlook and approach could help to curb the proliferation of bribe-collectors for illegal entry into a sovereign state.

9.3 Turning economic disaster into opportunity

The NDP frequently refers to 'an inclusive regional economic growth'. This theme could be used as a launch pad for further ideas to be explored in finding practical ways to stimulate Africa's regional economies. The story of China becoming a global economic player on account of offering one of the world's lowest labour costs deserves attention. South Africa is currently a member of the BRICS economic bloc where China is also represented. It is no rocket science that China was engaged in cheap-labour by the Chinese in China. Since South Africa and many African countries are on speaking terms with this Asian behemoth, we could find out how exactly the Chinese pulled this off. Perhaps there is a way to eliminate the attached worker and human rights abuses that arise within a cheap labour system. Let us imagine a fantastic Africa where the manufacturing sector is placed on a boom trajectory through beneficiating many of our products within the continent as opposed to exporting raw materials worth millions of jobs. We should briefly salivate on how pleasant it would feel to have the bulk of our textile products made in an African country. We have already shared some ideas that low wages could be acceptable in a financially transparent worker-employer relationship. We have further shown the devastation caused by foreign cheap labour on any country's job market and economy. We have however, not yet explored the possible benefits of cheap labour by cheap labourers in their own countries, similar to the China case but without human rights abuses.

We have indirectly exposed the existence of businesses in South Africa with an affinity for cheap foreign labour. Theoretically, we could determine which specific industries migrants are employed into and create a portfolio of businesses which could be encouraged to establish offshore operations. The poorest economies on the continent should receive priority in such cross-border investment drives. Given the already high indebtedness of African countries, it would be wise for African states to now stop securing finance from non-African entities. The African Union (AU) should exclusively facilitate funding and other mechanisms to support programmes aimed at lifting stranded economies on the continent. The AU funds could be accessed as low interest loans or limited grants used to subsidise low wages for cheap native labourers. Loans from the AU should be regarded as better than loans from outside the continent, as local funding is more like start-up finance from close family members. Collateral for such loans could come in the form of land or mining rights because such an arrangement still ensures that African assets remain in African hands in the event of defaults on repayments. The affected sovereign state would also have to be encouraged to provide significant incentives to attract more foreign direct investments. The corporations involved would also have to make sacrifices to behave in a socially responsible manner towards local communities. All loan and finance conditions imposed by the AU should be deliberately designed to be better than austerity measures imposed by global financiers. This approach would only stand a chance to succeed if the continent's political leadership accepts that their economies collapse mainly due to corruption and looting by the ruling minority class. The above stance should set the tone for African leaders to commit themselves to the highest moral standards that befit government office. The AU as the main investment partner would also need to provide expertise from the best minds on the continent to ensure that joint economic ventures survive from teething stages to being self-sustaining powerhouses.

9.4 The Pareto Principle – 'The Future of Activism'

The Pareto Principle is named after the Italian economist and engineer Vilfredo Pareto who towards the end of the 19th century observed that 80% of the effects within a system come from 20% of the causes. The Pareto Principle commonly referred to as the 80/20 rule has widely been proven to be true in life experiences in general and specifically in political life. Within political systems, the fate of the majority is generally seen to be left in the hands of a minority. This rule does not only ring true for undesirable events as it is also valid in useful optimisation themes. For example, it would be a nightmare to attempt having a productive meeting with millions of citizens than a few representatives. The following observations should stimulate a risk assessment debate on the actions of the minority measured against the actual will of the majority:

a) Voting for political party presidency in SA begins with all branch members voting for their preferred candidates. The list then goes to a provincial executive body comprising of fewer members, to be further shortened. The final short-listed candidates get delivered by a few provincial delegates who get to vote at the national elective conference. The provincial delegates are thus entrusted to deliver the candidate(s) chosen by branch members to the elective conference. If this minority of provincial delegates get persuaded to deviate from the original branch mandate, then a less favoured candidate could end up being elected and democracy subverted.

b) In South Africa, voting for the country's president is achieved through national elections where a desired political party gets voted in by adult citizens. So, millions of citizens would effectively outsource their voting mandate to a political party with fewer members (maybe less than 1 million). The party that gets majority votes would then present a president for the country through the process described in paragraph (a) above. This means that all the risk factors that befall the minority in process (a) would eventually affect the entire country.

c) In business, the decisions to determine wage levels within corporations are made by a minority of executives. Many such decisions have created an ever-increasing pay-gap between the same executives and the majority of workers who do not afford minimum living standards. The decision to hire cheap labour is made by an employer who chooses to make decent or even super profits at the expense of many slave workers.

d) It is the corruption and incompetence of a minority of black political leaders which endorse negative stereotypes and generalisations that black people are not capable of managing their own affairs.

e) It was a minority of white political leaders who designed and institutionalised the racist apartheid theme which to this day, continues to haunt and stigmatise many white people as anti-black.

f) Societies in general are seen to have comfortably delegated the role of social activism to a minority of NGOs and other entities. While these formations do all the research and hard work to hold those in power accountable, the risk of any minority getting persuaded to deviate from good causes to harm the majority, remains.

It is clear from the above excerpts that the majority which is mainly comprised of ordinary people without state or financial power must collectively push back against all forms of injustice. Otherwise, we all get to inherit lifelong stigmas and negative stereotypes on account of unsavoury kindred minorities. The time is ripe for the majority to rise because the minority will fail to consistently please many.

9.5 Truth and Reconciliation Commission (TRC)

It is a good decision to hit the reset button when faced with a situation where too many things go wrong at the same time. Many electronic gadgets come with a reset option which clears all user modifications, to revert the item back to the original clean factory settings. The TRC was constitutionally mandated to find reconciliatory solutions for victims and perpetrators of apartheid atrocities in South Africa. The thinking behind the TRC was for perpetrators to tell the whole truth and for victims to consider forgiveness and possible reparations as opposed to seeking revenge. The commissioners would then make decisions on available amnesty and reparation options. Reconciliation without implementable measures towards redress to correct exclusionary policies would still be worthless to the previously victimised communities (Kuokkanen, 2020).

Widespread anger among the previously subjugated communities in

SA needed to be accurately appraised and communicated. It then became common course that marginalised people were angry at the violence and dispossession supported through apartheid laws. Sanctions towards perpetrators were suspended in favour of forgiveness to pave the way for reconciliation (Aumann and Cogley, 2019). The fact that South Africa has not had any civil war since democracy attests to some success of the TRC, and the avoidance of a civil war is a massive achievement by any standard. One could further argue that if there was no TRC, then SA might have had the longest dragging court cases to try to identify and prosecute everyone responsible for apartheid crimes. The financial burden on the democratic state to prosecute all apartheid criminals could have been significant. The reconciliation project may therefore have saved significant South African resources and lives. We have been into this democracy for over 26 years and it turns out that some among those in leadership positions could be involved in corruption within the state and private entities in South Africa. The current immigration crisis should also be viewed as the cumulative symptom of corrupt activities both in SA and the native countries of immigrants.

South Africa's democratic state is faced with the question of spending billions in the pursuit of those alleged to have pocketed coins. We are further confronted with the possibility that many or all senior government leaders could be implicated in graft, in which case any investigative effort by the same accused could simply be seen as a smoke screen. In the event that successful prosecutions are obtained, we are still unlikely to fully recover what was stolen instead we would have to house and feed the same perpetrators within an already overcrowded correctional system.

The observed desire among Africans to impose maximum punishment for wrongdoing by fellow Africans is an interesting phenomenon. The continent was colonised for more than 300 years, so we should accept that it is absurdity for Africans to think that they could turn that wheel to realise full social and economic emancipation in the first 50 years of independence. It was also extreme ambition to have expected African leaders, who are themselves victims of colonial deprivation, to suddenly be perfect and without sin in their handling of Africa's newly found independence and massive resources. For many centuries of colonial rule, the colonisers themselves could not perfect their colonial agenda yet we do not see mass protests among western citizens demanding all past presidents and politicians who presided over colonies to be found and dealt with.

Africans need to forgive themselves for being the now-generation tasked with raising this continent from ashes to greatness. Africans can rule themselves and make this continent a global force to be reckoned with. We first deserve to give ourselves reasonable time after being separated for hundreds of years, to get familiar with our collective morality which should guide us in how we should properly handle our sisterhood and resources. Let us explore a TRC 2.0 where all who have committed wrongdoing get invited to tell all in exchange for amnesty with attached conditions, such as an affordable fine and a sanction (similar to a suspended sentence) to deter the re-occurrence of the same offences. We successfully forgave colonialism and apartheid criminality that pillaged our country for hundreds of years, so it should not be impossible to forgive grand theft in the last 26 years of democracy. The main achievement in this approach would be to relief pressure from a new democratic state to focus on rebuilding the economy and attending to pressing societal and continental needs. Failure to forgive ourselves would be tantamount to an inability to understand the dynamics of growth, underpinned by time and space. For any seed to grow into fruit-bearing maturity, it must be planted in a conducive space and be afforded time to be nurtured accordingly. The nurturing also involves removing opportunistic weeds without uprooting the plant itself. If we do not at least ponder this option as black people, then we need to seriously get our heads checked for still being heavily invested in the unity and reconciliation between black and white communities in SA. Black liberation movements, who currently form part of governing South Africa, deserve state-sponsored forgiveness, unity and reconciliation for the mistakes and crimes committed in the last 26 years. All black leaders who have been implicated in the last 26 years must ask for this forgiveness and stop hating themselves. 'Forgive us our debts as we also have forgiven our debtors'. Surely anyone can ask for forgiveness, especially those who forgive others (Biblica Inc., 2011). If our politicians would stop taking citizens for fools and humble themselves, then this nation could be open to forgive. Whenever we fall, and indeed we shall fall many times in our lives, it will always be our God given human right to rise and start afresh. Politics aside, a united multi-party government should be good for all South Africans and the continent at large.

9.6 Devolution of state power

For society to embrace the reconciliation proposition outlined above there must be a compelling incentive to the majority of South Africans who happen to be ordinary citizens not in any way implicated in state corruption. The state can be forgiven yet citizens might have reason to doubt that apologies would translate into subsequent good behaviour. Some of the state power which currently rests in a president may have to be devolved to citizens because centralised power is seen to be easily corruptible to serve minority interests among the ruling elite. An incentive that may prove hard to resist, could be the urgent development of legislation for a referendum to be held every two and a half years (30 months) to test whether communities still want a sitting president to continue as head of state. This approach could serve to alleviate fears amongst the electorate who experience gross abuses by a state yet have to wait for five years (60 months) to elect a new leader of government. Referendum laws could also be deliberately crafted to compel the state to seek the approval of citizens in a variety of big-ticket items such as:

- ❖ Massive procurement of arms
- ❖ Massive procurement of road e-tolling systems
- ❖ Awarding of mining rights for all sovereign mineral resources
- ❖ State procurement on large-scale projects which exceed specified funding thresholds
- ❖ Changes on legislation affecting morally contested issues.

It is only when citizens are involved in some of the historically far-reaching and contentious decisions by the state, that the country would realise a true government of the people by the people.

9.7 Summarising comments

- ➔ The ruling party has realised significant achievements since democracy.
- ➔ The sovereignty of SA should be handled in a manner that benefits all citizens not a few leaders.
- ➔ South Africa could benefit from a TRC for crimes committed in the last 26 years.
- ➔ Citizens must never outsource their activism role to a few others.

10. Concluding remarks

All immigration-related rage in South Africa should be directed at the Presidency and not immigrants. We have shown in previous sections how Ministers and other leaders have attempted to speak out against irregular migration to little avail. As custodians of all law and official statistical reports, the Presidency should step up and fix South Africa's immigration mess and salvage this country's sovereignty!

Ordinary people must stop using politically originated squabbles to attack each other while politicians are left to just sit and enjoy the violent show. This is important because the unity of citizens in this country and the continent should be a priority among citizens. We need each other to compel our elected leaders to serve us as we deserve or be removed! Politicians have proven over time that they can make a lot of sweet sounding promises which often result in no action but the pursuit of selfish agendas. Our commonalities which stem from mutual respect, moral conduct and cooperation will enable the creation of peaceful diverse communities for ourselves and the coming generations.

South Africa has a fair share of its own poor people and those who are officially allowed to share her limited resources, should do so sparingly and avoid binging which would obviously lead to tensions.

The country also needs a president who will rise against irregular migration as a matter of principle and law, not only during election campaigns especially:

❖ When ministers warn him on strained resources.
❖ When law enforcement gets attacked by illegal traders.
❖ When police officers get slain by illegal migrants.
❖ When citizens get killed by illegal migrants.
❖ When the job market displaces his jobless citizens in favour of cheap migrant labour.
❖ When expensive infrastructure gets destroyed by illegal migrants.
❖ When official statistics warn him on slave conditions in workplaces.
❖ When his sovereign state gets undermined by those who enter and do as they please as in 'no man's land'.

As we allow the leadership to address all concerns raised, let us join hands together with all diaspora formations to foster a culture of respect for host country sovereign laws and all human beings in our space. We should take a firm collective stand against all criminality to illicit the best possible migration experience for both hosts and guests.

11. References

Abiodun Alao (2012). Mugabe and the politics of security in Zimbabwe. Montreal: Mcgill-Queen's University Press.

Abraham, G.Y. (2020). A post-colonial perspective on African education systems. *African Journal of Education and Practice, 5(3), pp. 40-54.*

Adesina, F. (2020). *Beyond Smuggling of food Products, we Closed Borders Due to Influx of arms and Hard Drugs, President Buhari Tells Akufo-Addo of Ghana.* Press release: Federal Republic of Nigeria

Advisory Panel on Land Reform and Agriculture (2019). *Final report of the Advisory Panel on Land Reform and Agriculture.* South Africa: APLRA

American Psychological Association. (2014). *The road to resilience.* Washington, DC: American Psychological Association

ANA (2020). *News Article: Zim community expresses anger at murder of Diepsloot cop Oupa Matjie*

AU (2000). *The Constitutive Act of the AU.*

AU (2018). *Protocol to the treaty establishing the African Economic Community relating to the free movement of persons, right of residence and right of establishment.*

Aumann, A.G; Cogley, Z. (2019). Forgiveness and the Multiple functions of anger. *Journal of Philosophy of Emotion, 1(1), p 44 – 71.*

Biblica Inc. (2011). Holy Bible: New International Version. Colorado: Biblica Inc.

Briscoe, I. (2008). *The Proliferation of 'the Parallel State'.* Madrid: FRIDE (Working paper 71)

Brown, R; Danson, M. (2008). Fresh Talent or Cheap Labour? Accession State Migrant Labour in the Scottish Economy. *Scottish Affairs, 64(summer 2008), pp. 37 – 52.*

Buhari, M. (2018). *Presidential Executive Order for planning and execution of projects, promotion of Nigerian content in contracts and science, engineering and technology.* President, Federal republic of Nigeria.

Butschek, S; Sauermann, J. (2019). The effect of employment protection on firms' worker selection. Bonn: IZA – Institute of Labour Economics

CEE (2020). *Media Statement: Employment and Labour on 20th Commission for Employment Equity (CEE) Annual report 2019/20*

Charles, M. (2019). Abjection, identity and the enigmatic message: embodied meanings and social constructions. *Journal of Psychosocial Studies, 12 (1&2), pp. 69 – 79.*

Chimbarange, A; Mukenge, C; Mutambwa, J. (2013). Image Repair: Analysis of President Robert Gabriel Mugabe's rhetoric following sanctions on Zimbabwe. *International Journal of Linguistics, 5(1)*

Corcoran, T; White, J; Riele, K; Baker, A; Moylan, P. (2019). Psychosocial justice for students in custody. *Journal of Psychosocial Studies, 12 (1&2), pp. 41 – 56.*

Craven, M. (2015). Between law and history: the Berlin Conference of 1884-1885 and the logic of free trade. London *Review of International Law, 3(1), pp. 31-59.*

DEL (2019). *Press release: Labour court gives thumbs up to Employment Equity following court challenge.* Pretoria: DEL

DHA (2017). *Media statement by Minister Gigaba on tensions between citizens and foreign nationals.* Pretoria: DHA

DEL (2019a). *Media statement: Employment and Labour Minister, TW Nxesi calls for 'tough hand' of the inspectorate to deal with unscrupulous employers.* Pretoria: DEL

DEL (2019b). *Media statement: Joint Statement of the Ministers addressing the ongoing spate of violence in the Road Freight and*

Logistic Sector. Pretoria: DEL

DEL (2020a). *Media statement: Dubious Spar employer ordered to pay millions of rands to workers for unlawful deductions, non-compliance with National Minimum Wage (NMW) and overtime among others.* Pretoria: DEL

DEL (2020b). *Media statement: JHB magistrates court to hear the application for leave to appeal the bail in the Chinese human trafficking and violation of SA labour laws case.* Pretoria: DEL

DEL (2020c). *Media statement: Road freight and logistics industry planned national shutdown.* Pretoria: DEL

DTIC (2019). *Media statement: B-BBEE Commission releases annual report on national status and trends on B-BBEE.*

Fagunwa, T. (2019). Ubuntu: Revisiting an endangered African philosophy in quest for a pan-Africanist revolutionary ideology. *Genealogy, 3, p. 45.*

Farah, R. (2020). Expat, Local and Refugee: 'Studying Up' the Global Division of Labor and Mobility in the Humanitarian Industry in Jordan. Migration in Society: *Advances in Research, 3(1), pp. 130 – 144.*

Fevre, R. (1984). *Cheap Labour and Racial Discrimination.* Aldershot: Gower.

Fox, J. (2012). *State Power and Clientelism. Clientelism in Everyday Latin American Politics, pp.187–211.*

GCIS (2016). 20 years of the years of the South African Constitution. *Insight, 1(23).*

Idemudia, E; Boehnke, K. (2020). Social Experiences of Migrants. *Social Indicators Research Series, pp.119–135.*

ILO (2013). *Decent work indicators: guidelines for producers and users of statistical and legal framework indicators.* Geneva: ILO

ILO (2015). *ILO global estimates of migrant workers and migrant domestic workers: results and methodology.* Geneva: ILO

ILO (2019a). 'ILO Response to Syrian Refugee Crisis in Jordan'. https://www.ilo.org/beirut/areasofwork/employment-policy/syrian-refugee-crisis/jordan/lang--en/ index.htm

ILO (2019b). *The future of work and migration: Thematic background paper for the 12th ASEAN Forum on Migrant Labour.* T hailand: ILO

ILO (2019c). *What works: promoting pathways to decent work. Geneva: ILO*

ILO (2020a). *ILO brief: Trade union action to promote fair recruitment for migrant workers.* Geneva: ILO

ILO (2020b). *In the shadow of the state: Recruitment and migration of South Indian women as domestic workers to the Middle East.* Geneva: ILO

ILO (2020c). *Recruitment fees and related costs: what migrant workers from Cambodia, the Lao People's Democratic Republic and Myanmar pay to work in Thailand.* Thailand: ILO

ILO (2020d). *Syrian refugees in the Turkish labour market.* Turkey: ILO

Joint Parliamentary Committees (2019). *The impact of illegal migration on cities: input from Joburg and Ekurhuleni mayors, SALGA and Minister of Home Affairs.* Cape town: Parliament

Jones, D.W. and Frost, E. (2020). Pandemics, governance and psychosocial thinking. *Journal of Psychosocial Studies, 13(2), pp.131–134.*

Kuokkanen, R. (2020). Reconciliation as a Threat or Structural Change? The Truth and Reconciliation Process and Settler Colonial Policy Making in Finland. *Human Rights Review, 21, pp. 293 – 312.*

Long, K; Crisp, J (2011). *In harm's way: the irregular movement of migrants to Southern Africa from the Horn and Great Lakes regions. New issues in refugee research, Research paper no. 200.* Geneva: UNHCR.

Madi, P.M. (2016). *Black Economic Empowerment: 20 years later – The baby and the bathwater.* Randburg: KR Publishing

Maharaj, M. (2008). *The ANC and South Africa's negotiated transition to democracy and peace.* Berlin: Berghof Research Center For Constructive Conflict Management.

Malawi (1997). *The Constitution of the Republic of Malawi, 1 of 1997.*

Malawi Government. *Functions of the Department of Immigration.*

Malisa, M.; Nhengeze, P. (2018). Pan-Africanism: A quest for liberation and the pursuit of a united Africa. *Genealogy 2018, 2(3), p 28.*

Mandelbaum, B. (2019). Unemployment: a psychoanalytic approach to families of unemployed workers. *Journal of Psychosocial Studies, 12 (1&2), pp. 57 – 67.*

Masterman-Smith, H; Elton, J. (2007). *Cheap labour: the Australian Way.* AIRAANZ Conference 2007, Association of Industrial Relations Academics of Australia and New Zealand, Auckland, 7-9 February.

Mbeki, T (2016). *South Africa's policy towards Zimbabwe: A synopsis.* Pretoria: Unisa

Mihály, Z. (2015). The Making of Cheap Labour Power: Nokia"s Case in Cluj. *Studia Universitatis Babes-Bolyai Sociologia, 6(1), pp.63–82.*

Ministry of Home Affairs, Zambia (2018). *Press statement on the need for public order as trading activities resume gradually in the city of Lusaka.* Lusaka: Republic of Zambia

Monakali, S; Mokgatle-Nthabu, M; Oguntibeju, O. (2011). Characteristics of abused women and factors that enhanced abuse. *Scientific Research and Essays, 6(22), pp. 4749 – 4761.*

Moseneke, D. (2016). *My own liberation.* Johannesburg: Picador Africa

National Planning Commission (2012). *National development plan, 2030: Our future - make it work.* Pretoria: National Planning Commission.

Ndlovu, SM; Strydom, M. (2016). *The Thabo Mbeki I know. Johannesburg:* Picador Africa.

Nigeria (1999). *The Constitution of the Federal Republic of Nigeria.*

OAU (1989). *Harare Declaration: Declaration of the OAU ad hoc committee on Southern Africa on the question of South Africa.* Harare: OAU

Pratt, J. (2020). *LAW, INSECURITY AND RISK CONTROL: neo-liberal governance and the populist revolt.* S.L.: Springer Nature.

Ramiz, A; Rock, P; Strang, H. (2020). Detecting Modern Slavery on Cannabis Farms: The Challenges of Evidence. Cambridge *Journal of Evidence-Based Policing, August 2020.*

SABC (2018). *News Article: Foreign nationals are burdening the SA health system: Motsoaledi.*

SAHRC (2016). *Final Report: African Diaspora Forum and others versus King Goodwill Zwelithini.*

SAHRC (2017). *Media Statement: SAHRC concerned by xenophobic statements of leaders.*

SAPS (2018). *Media Statement from the Office of the Deputy Minister of Police: Participation of the Deputy Minister of Police in SAHRC Mediation Process.* Pretoria: SAPS

SAPS (2019a). *Media Statement by the Ministry of Police: Police Minister General Bheki Cele allays the concerns of the country's business community in the wake of mass violence and destruction in Gauteng.*

SAPS (2019b). *Media Statement from the Office of the Eastern Cape Provincial Commissioner: Three trucks damaged during national truck strike in Motherwell and Paterson.*

SAPS (2019c). *Media Statement from the Office of the Gauteng Provincial Commissioner: Police retreat from attackers in Johannesburg CBD to avert bloodshed.*

Sefalafala, T. (2020). Incorporating bo-mahlalela: reconceptualising unemployment and labour in the age of uncertainty and fear. *South African Labour Bulletin, 43 (4).*

Smudde, P.M; Courtright, J.L (2008). Time to get a job: Helping Image Repair Theory begin a career in business. *Public Relations Journal 2008, 2(1)*

South Africa (1995a). *Labour Relations Act 66 of 1995.*

South Africa (1995b). *Promotion of national unity and reconciliation Act 34 of 1995*

South Africa (1996). *The Constitution of the Republic of South Africa.*

South Africa (1997a). *Basic Conditions of Employment Act 75 of 1997.*

South Africa (1997b). *Housing Act 107 of 1997.*

South Africa (1998a). *Employment Equity Act 55 of 1998.*

South Africa (1998b). *The National Environmental Management Act 107 of 1998.*

South Africa (2000). *Preferential Procurement Policy Framework Act 5 of 2000*

South Africa (2002a). *Defence Act 42 of 2002.*

South Africa (2002b). *Immigration Act 13 of 2002.*

South Africa (2003a). *Broad Based Black Economic Empowerment Act 53 of 2003.*

South Africa (2003b). *Traditional Leadership and Governance Framework Act 41 of 2003.*

South Africa (2004). *Immigration Amendment Act 19 of 2004*

South Africa (2011). *Immigration Amendment Act 13 of 2011*

South Africa (2013). *Broad Based Black Economic Empowerment Amendment Act 46 of 20013*

South Africa (2013). *Employment Equity Amendment Act 47 of 2013*

South Africa (2014). *Employment Services Act 4 of 2014*

South Africa (2017). *Preferential Procurement Regulations, 2017.*

StatsSA (2018). *Quarterly Labour Force Survey: 4th Quarter of 2017.* Pretoria: Statistics South Africa.

StatsSA (2019). *Labour market outcomes of migrant populations in South Africa, 2012 and 2017.* Pretoria: Statistics South Africa.

Steinmetz, C.H.D. (2013). Immigrants and Expats. *Pan European Networks, 8, pp. 66-67.*

Steinmetz, C.H.D. (2015). *Supporting elderly expats & immigrants: Logistical and psychological problems.* Amsterdam: Expats & Immigrants B.V Consultancy.

Tanesini, A. (2020). Arrogance, Polarisation and Arguing to Win - in Alessandra Tanesini and Michael P. Lynch (eds), Polarisation, Arrogance, and Dogmatism: Philosophical Perspectives, London: Routledge, pp. 158-74.

UN (1989). *Declaration on Apartheid and its Destructive Consequences in Southern Africa.* New York: UN

UN (1948). *Universal Declaration of Human Rights.* Paris: UN

UN (2006). *The core international human rights treaties.* New York: UN.

UN (2015). *Transforming our world: Agenda 2030 for Sustainable Development.* New York: UN General Assembly

UN (2018). *Over 330,000 Congolese migrants at risk after mass deportations from Angola – UN human rights chief.* Geneva: UN

News

Van Breda, A. (2019). Developing the notion of Ubuntu as African theory for social work practice. *Social Work, 55(4)*

Watermayer R; Phillips S. (2020). *Public infrastructure delivery and construction sector dynamism in the South African economy: Public discussion draft.* South Africa: National Planning Commission

Weisberg, R.W. (1993). *Creativity: beyond the myth of genius.* New York: W.H. Freeman.

Zaamout, N.M. (2020). Post-colonialism and Security. The Palgrave *Encyclopaedia of Global Security Studies, pp.1–5.* Palgrave Macmillan.

Zimbabwe (2007). *Indigenisation and Economic Empowerment Act 14 of 2007.*

Zimbabwe (2013). *Constitution of Zimbabwe Amendment Act 20 of 2013.*

www.ingramcontent.com/pod-product-compliance
Lightning Source LLC
Chambersburg PA
CBHW050352280326
41933CB00010BA/1432